D1103723

Living Jesus' Way

Everyday Principles for a New Life

CHRIS HAZELIP

WESTBOW
PRESS®
A DIVISION OF THOMAS NELSON
& ZONDERVAN

THE HOLY BIBLE, NEW INTERNATIONAL VERSION®, NIV® Copyright © 1973,
1978, 1984, 2011 by Biblica, Inc.® Used by permission. All rights reserved worldwide.

Scripture taken from the NEW AMERICAN STANDARD BIBLE®,
Copyright © 1960,1962,1963,1968,1971,1972,1973,1975,1977,19
95 by The Lockman Foundation. Used by permission.

WestBow Press books may be ordered through booksellers or by contacting:

WestBow Press
A Division of Thomas Nelson & Zondervan
1663 Liberty Drive
Bloomington, IN 47403
www.westbowpress.com
1 (866) 928-1240

ISBN: 978-1-5127-7017-9 (sc)
ISBN: 978-1-5127-7018-6 (hc)
ISBN: 978-1-5127-7016-2 (e)

Library of Congress Control Number: 2016921356

For more information on the author, please visit www.chrishazelip.com

Print information available on the last page.

WestBow Press rev. date: 02/16/2017

CONTENTS

ACKNOWLEDGMENTS

To my wife, Sally: *"That you and I could live our lives at the same time on earth—how incredible God's plan."* Do you think Flavia ever realized she wrote that for us! I love you, babe. You've made me a better man, and I am forever grateful.

To my children, Christianna, Carly, Christopher, and Collin: You got some of the best of me and some of the worst of me, and I'm not sure which drives me the most crazy. I thank God that it all blends into a unique "you," and it gives me great joy to sign my texts and e-mails, "Love, Dad," and mean it.

To my parents: It never seems to turn out the way we would draw it up, but through it all, love somehow remains. Thanks for all you sacrificed for Michele, Nicole, and me, and letting us always know we were loved.

To my editor, Sandra Hedrick: Your scalpel is as sharp and thorough as it is loving, and I am so grateful for you. Thanks for helping me see.

To the pastor-teachers in my life, past through present, Gene Jenkins, Rod Bunton, Mike Braun, Jon Krug, Tim Lusk, Doug Rutt, Dennis Bratton, and Jason Cullum: Worthy shepherds all, your impact on me remains great. Thank you. **κήρυξον τὸν λόγον**

To our Sunday Morning Class: your open minds are almost as precious to me as your open hearts. Thanks for your encouragement and love. It is my privilege to be called your "teacher."

Chris Hazclip
Jacksonville, Florida

INTRODUCTION

This book can change your life. That is not hyperbole—it is a fact. It has nothing to do with the writing prowess of the author and everything to do with the person and teachings of Jesus. Whoever you are, whatever your life circumstance, whatever your past or baggage, whatever your personality, you can change now. You may be free or incarcerated, rich, poor, or middle-class. You may be a capitalist, socialist, or communist. You could be a Democrat, Republican, Libertarian, or without party affiliation. You might live in a relatively free society or under the most oppressive, totalitarian regime. You might be married, single, or divorced, straight, gay, bisexual, or transgendered. Anyone and everyone can experience the profound life-change of following Jesus. No one is barred—whoever wills may come.

Since Jesus first shared his way to live, millions of people from all walks of life, all political persuasions, all socioeconomic conditions, all sexual orientations, every race, ethnicity, or national origin, throughout every time, epoch, or era have been living proof that his teachings are positively life changing. If you decide to live the way Jesus taught, your life circumstances may or may not change, but the change in you will be immediate and noticeable by those who know you. And, in the midst of your circumstances, however challenging or trying, whether they are the consequence of your own choices, the choices of others inflicted upon you, or a combination of both, you will experience peace, joy, love, and hope. Think about that! Isn't that what you really long for? Moreover, your character will, over time, exhibit patience, kindness, goodness, self-control, and other universally valued qualities.

No preparation is necessary, nor is there a prerequisite "house cleaning." By starting this day doing even one thing because Jesus said, "Do it," or refraining from one thing because he said, "Don't do it," your life-change will begin. Interested? Then read on.

CHAPTER 1

True Believers

Said I'm a believer, yeah, yeah, yeah
—The Monkees

If you have ever backpacked off-trail in a dense, rugged forest, using a compass and topographic map, you know the importance of a proper bearing. There is little hope of reaching a day's destination, often a vital water source, without having an accurate bearing and following it closely. If you are only slightly off—even a degree or two—over the course of a full day, you will miss where you are trying to go.

While in college, long before the days of GPS, I spent two weeks "bush whacking" in the Northwoods of Michigan and became familiar with contour lines, which reflect the elevation of the terrain by how close those lines appear on the map. The greater the elevation change, the closer the contour lines. After a few days in the woods, identifying where you are on the map is no easy task, and involves looking intently for features in the surrounding terrain that might be unique, such as a berm, cliff or sudden change in elevation, and then trying to match that to the map's squiggly contour lines. Once you interpret where you are, you can set the bearing on the compass and head to your next destination. If you are wrong about the starting point, however, it does not matter how skillfully you follow your bearing. At the end of the day, you are still lost.

Few of us would dispute that in life, where we are and where we are headed are important issues, worthy of our serious attention. And, just as with a backpacker in the woods, our own real, human experiences teach us that both make a critical difference in our lives.

Jesus had a lot to say about direction in life. He called himself "the way" and extended the simple invitation to his first disciples, "Follow me." This essential call remained the same from the beginning of his three-year ministry to the end and, importantly, was made to anybody who would listen no matter what his or her starting point. The Bible gives account of him inviting all manner of people to follow him, including those who were rich, poor, religious, pagan, sick, disabled, well, popular, or despised, and they consisted of business or community leaders, widows, soldiers, and ordinary working class folks. Whatever their lot, circumstance, or place in life, Jesus held himself out as the "bearing" they should follow from right where they were.

So what does it mean to follow Jesus? Sometimes we think or act as if it is merely *assenting to* some *propositions* about him. Jesus is reported to have made many claims regarding himself that, if true, are earth-shaking, and it is no wonder that they have captivated some of the greatest minds in humanity for over twenty centuries. For example, he claimed to be the Messiah promised in the Old Testament (John 4:25–26), God's son (Matthew 16:16–17), co-equal with God (John 10:30), existing from eternity past (John 8:57–58), and to have the power to forgive sins (Matthew 9:2). Not only that, the accounts of Jesus' life describe many mind-boggling miracles that he performed and then talked about in encounters with his adversaries and supporters alike. Some churches and people who identify themselves as Christ-followers proclaim that the essential quality of being a Christian is acknowledging "spiritual laws" or other correct statements about Jesus and his life.

But Jesus made clear that his genuine followers are characterized by something else. Claiming that the words he brought are literally a message from his Father God (John 14:24, 7:16), Jesus said that those who *believe* in him and *love* him are those who take his words seriously and do what he says (John 14:12, 21, 24). Such people are his friends (John 15:14). True believers do the works that Jesus lived his life doing (John 14:12), meaning not that we must duplicate his miracles, but rather that we must live our lives *the way he lived* his own. And Jesus reminds us that we have opportunity to do this even greater than he since his life was about to be cut short after just thirty-three years (ibid.). Christ-followers recognize and respond to Jesus' teachings as what he claimed they were: words from God concerning how we are to live.

This is a very serious matter and is reiterated by Jesus throughout his recorded ministry:

> Not everyone who says to me, "Lord, Lord," will enter the kingdom of heaven, but only the one who does the will of my Father who is in heaven. Many will say to me on that day, "Lord, Lord, did we not prophesy in your name and in your name drive out demons and in your name perform many miracles?" Then I will tell them plainly, 'I never knew you. Away from me, you evildoers!' Therefore everyone who hears these words of mine and puts them into practice is like a wise man who built his house on the rock. The rain came down, the streams rose, and the winds blew and beat against that house; yet it did not fall, because it had its foundation on the rock. (Matthew 7:21–25)

Even the Great Commission that Jesus gave his followers to "go and make disciples, baptizing them in the name of the Father and of the Son and of the Holy Spirit," includes the central thought that his disciples are those who "obey everything that [he] taught" (Matthew 28:19–20).

Jesus has shown us the way to live—how God wants and made us to live. To be followers of Jesus, then and now, we must embrace life his way by practicing the principles that he modeled and taught. If we are not pursuing his way of life, we are *not* followers of Christ. As the apostle John put it,

> We know that we have come to know him if we keep his commands. Whoever says, "I know him," but does not do what he commands is a liar, and the truth is not in that person. But if anyone obeys his word, love for God is truly made complete in them. This is how we know we are in him: Whoever claims to live in him must live as Jesus did. (1 John 2:3–6)

In fact, the scriptures show that if we correctly recognize *who* Jesus is without following his teachings, it does not even make us distinguishable from those known as "demons."

> When he arrived at the other side in the region of the Gadarenes, two demon-possessed men coming from the tombs met him. They were so violent that no one could pass that way. "What do you want with us, Son of God?" they shouted. "Have you come here to torture us before the appointed time?" (Matthew 8:28–29)

As early church leaders taught,

> In the same way, faith by itself, if it is not accompanied by action, is dead. But someone will say, "You have faith; I have deeds." Show me your faith without deeds, and I will show you my faith by my deeds. You believe that there is one God. Good! Even the demons believe that —and shudder. (James 2:17–19)

Empty words, even the right words, rarely impress us—it should be no surprise that they also do not impress God.

Sometimes people who claim to be Christ-followers can fool others and even themselves. There are crooks and con men in churches trying to fleece vulnerable and trusting people, typically in financial or sexual ways. That reality has plagued the church since its earliest days and is the subject of several pointed scriptural warnings (2 Peter 2:3; 13–14; 2 Timothy 3:6). Throughout the history of the Christian church, phonies have lurked like wolves in sheep's clothing. What's more alarming than being duped by another, however, is self-deception, where people who have perhaps convinced themselves they are Jesus' followers will discover instead that he never knew them (Matthew 7:23). The apostle Paul therefore encouraged self-examination:

> Examine yourselves to see whether you are in the faith; test yourselves. Do you not realize that Christ Jesus is in you—unless, of course, you fail the test? And I trust

that you will discover that we have not failed the test. (2 Corinthians 13:5–6)

So what is it that distinguishes the true believer from the one who is seeking to deceive others or caught in the throes of self-deception? Again, Jesus said it is doing the will of God. "Not everyone who says to me, 'Lord, Lord,' will enter the kingdom of heaven, but only the one who does the will of my Father who is in heaven" (Matthew 7:21). He stated that this was also his purpose: "For I have come down from heaven not to do my will but to do the will of him who sent me" (John 6:38), and characteristic of those in his family: "For whoever does the will of my Father in heaven is my brother and sister and mother" (Matthew 12:50).

This is not a salvation-by-works message. The startling and liberating news of the gospel is that we are saved by God's grace through faith. We cannot *earn* God's favor or acceptance—it is an undeserved gift (Romans 6:23; Ephesians 2:8–9). Jesus' teaching, reiterated throughout the New Testament, is that being in a genuine relationship with God is, and always has been, based on faith. But real faith is *always* revealed and confirmed in the way we live our lives; that is, faith without works is dead (James 2:17, 22).

Not only is living life the way Jesus taught the hallmark of his true followers, it will also, he promised, profoundly affect our *experience* of life. When we practice living his way, Jesus assures us that we will have strength in the inevitable storms of life despite our human vulnerability (Matthew 7:24–25). We will experience *true* life, one enlightened to the way our Creator designed us to live so that we no longer need to wander in the dark (John 8:12). Life lived Jesus' way is abundant and full (John 10:10), and results in us being "blessed and happy" (Matthew 5:1–11), filled with an inner *joy* that is "complete" (John 15:10–11). It is life with a revitalized spirit, like being "newly reborn" (John 3:5–8), and is spiritual in its source (John 6:63). This is life with an eternal quality wherein *we know God* (John 17:3). And pursuing life Jesus' way brings *peace*, no matter what troubles or challenges we might face:

I have told you these things, so that in me you may have peace. In this world you will have trouble. But take heart! I have overcome the world. (John 16:33)

Remarkably, life can be lived Jesus' way, whatever our starting point or life circumstances. It is and has been lived by people who are rich or poor, sick or well, young or old, captive or free, of every race and on every continent, irrespective of country and political or economic systems, so that the assembly of genuine Christ-followers is beautifully diverse, comprised of all manner of people from every tribe, nation, and tongue.

Perhaps you have reached the point at which you are looking for a new way to live your life—a way that is time-tested and has been found true, effective and worthy by countless others. Whoever you are and whatever you have done or failed to do, there is available to you a way filled with purpose, hope, love, joy, and peace. Jesus said he is that way. His message is as relevant today as when he proclaimed it. The way he taught and showed us to live echoes down through the ages as an unforgettable life given in demonstration of what it means to live God's way. It is the way life works best and the way we were designed by God to live it. And the promise is that you and I can start living like this *now.* Your life or mine could be characterized by the most awful choices and dysfunction in the past and even up until this moment, but we can finish reading this page changed, renewed, and on a different path, headed in a new direction. In George MacDonald's challenging words,

> Get up, and do something the master tells you. The moment you do, you instantly make yourself his disciple. Instead of asking yourself whether you believe or not, ask yourself whether you have this day done one thing because he said, "Do it," or once abstained because he said, "Do not do it." …It is simply absurd to say you believe, or even want to believe in him, if you do not do anything he tells you. (MacDonald 2008, 213)

So how does one live Jesus' way? Let's explore that together.

CHAPTER 2

Loving God

You move me. I can't go with you and stay where I am
So you move me.
—Pierce Pettis

Early in my legal career, I was helping one of our firm's senior partners with a jury trial in federal court. One of the hardest things for me to do as a trial lawyer, especially then in my youthful exuberance, is to sit as second chair to the lead trial counsel. In that role, my job, at least during the parts of the trial that would take place in front of the jury, was primarily to provide support for my boss. I was to be aware of everything that was going on and to anticipate, recognize, and be fully prepared to address legal issues that could arise in a moment's notice.

When the stern federal judge entered the courtroom to the bailiff's cry, "All rise!" and court was called into session, I was eager and nervous, ready to enter the fray after months of preparation.

The judge said, "Be seated," and then looked to us at our table and asked "Counsel, are you ready to proceed?"

I leaped back to my feet even as my boss was standing up and exclaimed "Yes, Your Honor!"

Somewhat diplomatically, but in no uncertain terms, my boss turned to me, cleared his throat, and said, "I've got this." With those three words, I was put in place, reminded that my role at trial would be to serve *him* as the lead lawyer and he did not need me to speak to the judge on behalf of our side. It was a humbling lesson that continues to surface in my life, but sometimes in different and unexpected ways.

I was more recently playing in a local club golf tournament involving two-man teams. Our opponents were left with an eight-to-ten foot putt to win the hole and match, and as the player who would be putting looked over the putt, his partner began giving advice as to how to play it. That sort of teamwork is common and often helpful and had taken place throughout the match. In this instance, however, the advice was cut off with those same three words, "I've got this," leaving the next moments tense and pregnant with awkward silence.

When we communicate verbally or by our actions, "I've got this," we are claiming a self-sufficiency that may or may not be warranted in a particular circumstance. We may be so certain, trained, or skilled in a particular task that the input of another is actually of no value to us and perhaps even distracting so as to take us off our games. If I am honest, however, this attitude reflects in me, more often than not, an arrogance proclaiming that I do not want or need another's help, even when sober thought would recognize that such help could be truly beneficial.

In a spiritual sense, with respect to the God who possesses the attributes described in the Bible, it is worthwhile to consider whether we can ever be truly self-sufficient, or is recognition of our need for God necessarily entailed in being what Jesus referred to as "poor in spirit" (Matthew 5:3)? Is professing one's dependence inherent in honoring God as God (Romans 1:21)? In other words, if God made us, can we ever legitimately tell Him, "I've got this?"

A lawyer is reported to have asked Jesus what is the most important command in the law of God, and Jesus replied, "Love the Lord your God with all your heart and with all your soul and with all your mind. This is the first and greatest commandment" (Matthew 22:36–38). In another report on this or a similar encounter, he adds the term "strength" (Mark 12:28–30), essentially encompassing with his answer the *Shema*, which was familiar to the Jewish audience.

All of these—heart, soul, mind, and strength—describe essential and inherent aspects of what it means to be alive and human, and there is no humanity without them. They are not listed separately in order to suggest that there are distinct compartments of our human condition that we can open or shut as we wish, loving God with one and not the others. With his answer, Jesus echoes Moses before him and illustrates the breadth of human experience so as to remind us that a person who truly loves God is *fully involved*. I am to love God with *all* of my being and with everything I've got. Moreover, Jesus' teaching that this is the "first and greatest commandment" means that such all-encompassing love for God is to be above and before all else. It must be the fundamental priority of my life.

That may sound good, but what does it look like? The command to love God in this way could seem to present a sanitized, sanctimonious approach to life that is unrealistic and unattainable. To be sure, religious people in Jesus' time and through the ages have presented it like that, often as a tool to control other people's lives by inflicting upon them a heavy burden or "yoke" of detailed and oppressive behavior standards. But this is not the picture of loving God that is given in the scriptures.

To explore that, it is helpful to consider scriptural references to these aspects of our human nature, starting with the heart, which, in the Hebrew culture of the inquiring lawyer, would likely be understood as the core of every human being from which our deepest convictions, beliefs, and volitional will come. Our hearts are where our *commitments* are made, and the scriptures emphasize being wholehearted in our love for God. It is those who seek God with all their hearts who find him (Jeremiah 29:13). Those who follow him wholeheartedly experience his blessing (Joshua 14:9). In fact, there are many examples given in the Bible of ways in which one's expression of love for God can be wholehearted, including service (1 Samuel 12:20), holding fast to him (Joshua 22:5), turning to him (Deuteronomy 30:10), returning to him (1 Samuel 7:3), obedience (Psalm 119:34), financial giving (1 Chronicles 29:9), trusting in him (Proverbs 3:5), praise (Psalm 86:12), giving thanks (Psalm 9:1), and calling upon him (Psalm 119:145). In all these ways, it is clear that loving God is not a half-hearted venture.

They also provide specific applications of what the scriptures refer to as wholehearted "devotion" to God, such as when King David prayed for his son Solomon, "Give my son Solomon the wholehearted devotion to keep your commands" (1 Chronicles 29:19), and when King Hezekiah, while in the throes of disease, asked God to extend his life, "Remember, Lord, how I have walked before you faithfully and with wholehearted devotion and have done what is good in your eyes" (2 Kings 20:3).

We see in both prayers a connection between obedience and loving God with one's whole heart. The scriptures, however, repeatedly offer King David as an example of one who was obedient to God, such as when young King Josiah "did what was right in the eyes of the Lord and followed completely the ways of his father David" (2 Kings 22:2), or when King Hezekiah "did what was right in the eyes of the Lord, just as his father David had done" (2 Chronicles 29:2). When King Solomon lost his wholehearted devotion to God and his kingdom of Israel was threatening to split in rebellion, the prophet Ahijah delivered this word from the Lord to Solomon's rival Jeroboam,

> But I will not take the whole kingdom out of Solomon's hand; I have made him ruler all the days of his life for the sake of David my servant, whom I chose and who obeyed my commands and decrees. (1 Kings 11:34)

This is striking because in addition to David's many good qualities, he notoriously stole another man's wife and had the man—a loyal and valiant warrior in his army—killed in an attempt to get away with it. Holding David up as an example of obedience to God probably reveals a lot, including important insights about the forgiving character of God. For our purposes here, however, it most certainly reminds us that loving God with all one's heart does not imply an unrealistic standard of perfection. Rather, it is a way of living that can be pursued in spite of our faults and even in the context of our wrong choices.

While the heart may represent the core of our beings, we know that there is much more that comprises our human natures. For instance, what about the seat of our emotions, the soul, from which we each can experience deep anguish, profound longing, overwhelming gratitude, or even transcendent joy? Most of us recognize the soul as that aspect of our beings that feels moved or responds, often through the touch of music, beauty, art and poetry. It is not a uniquely spiritual concept, but one shared and recognized throughout humanity, including among those who have no present interest in God. It would seem quite natural, would it not, that being in relationship with the God who made us would involve the devotion of our hearts *and* souls? Indeed, David encouraged the leaders of

Israel, "Now devote your heart and soul to seeking the LORD your God" (1 Chronicles 22:19).

I once heard Dr. Philip Ryken, president of Wheaton College (IL), observe, "God's redemptive work is never just a drama; it's a *musical*" (Ryken 2014). When you think about it, there are several scriptural accounts from beginning to end illustrating that this is so, including Moses' song after the Israelites were delivered through the Red Sea (Exodus 15:1); Mary's song after Gabriel's announcement that she would give birth to the Savior of the world (Luke 1:46); and the "Revelation song" that the redeemed will sing in eternity (Revelation 5:13). It is also recognized in exhortations to early Christ-followers to "sing and make music from your heart to the Lord" (Ephesians 5:19) and "sing to God with gratitude in your hearts" (Colossians 3:16). The poet W. H. Auden captured the essence of such soul responses when he wrote:

> I know nothing, except what everyone knows—if there
> when Grace dances, I should dance. (Auden 1991, 743)

While scriptures including the Psalms are certainly filled with such singing and dancing (as well as poetry and the playing of various musical instruments) in timeless expressions of awe, rejoicing, and praise, we cannot ignore that they also include other emotional outpourings of the human soul such as anger, sorrow, lament, and question-filled doubt. These, too, are true to our experiences in a fallen world, and it would be difficult to imagine any genuine search for or relationship with God without such cries from the depth of one's soul.

Consider also scriptural accounts of Martha's sister, Mary, anointing Jesus' feet with costly perfume and wiping them with her hair and tears (John 12:1–3), or David's description of his soul as "thirsty" for God (Psalm 63:1), or Jesus' reference to those who "hunger and thirst for righteousness" as blessed and happy because of the quenching that will come (Matthew 5:6). These are examples of people loving God with all their souls, who, at least in those moments, reflect a *longing* for God and life pursued His way. The inescapable truth reverberating throughout the pages of the Bible, and experienced in the lives of countless witnesses who have gone before us and surround us even today, is that loving God also involves an emotional commitment welling up from the depth of our beings.

The engagement of our minds is essential, as well, and undoubtedly tied to a wholehearted devotion to God. As David told his son, Solomon,

> And you, my son Solomon, acknowledge the God of your father, and serve him with wholehearted devotion and with a willing mind, for the Lord searches every heart and understands every desire and every thought. (1 Chronicles 28:9)

The ancient psalmist recognized that we are blessed and firmly grounded as people when we contemplate or meditate on God and His standards for living (i.e., the Law of the Lord), which actually brings us delight (Psalm 1:2–3) and peace (Isaiah 26:3). In the New Testament, the apostle Paul urged us to demolish thoughts that are set up against God and to instead capture every thought for obedience to Jesus (2 Corinthians 10:5). He also reminded us that what we think about is extremely important, and we are encouraged to devote our minds to what is right, noble, pure, excellent, and true (Philippians 4:8).

Sometimes Christians are categorically portrayed as unthinking, but such a criticism is undermined by simple reflection on the many Christ-followers through the ages who are widely recognized for their intellectual brilliance and creativity. For example, the apostle Paul had a sterling academic pedigree as a student of the noted Rabbi Gamaliel (Acts 22:3), and was a skilled and effective debater. With his powerful mind, he attracted the attention of intelligent people (Acts 13:7), and boldly took on sceptics and critics alike in various religious and secular settings, persuading many (Acts 14:1, 17:12). In that context, Paul showed that he was well-versed in the writers and poets of his day (Acts 17:28), and his claims withstood testing and critical examination (Acts 17:11).

Of course, there are many other examples of brilliant and creative people spanning the millennia, from Augustine of Hippo to Thomas Aquinas, Nicholas Copernicus to Isaac Newton, Michelangelo to J. S. Bach, Blaise Pascal to James Clerk Maxwell, Soren Kierkegaard to Reinhold Niebuhr, C. S. Lewis to Os Guinness, Dorothy Sayer to

Marilynne Robinson, Flannery O'Connor to Madeleine L'Engle, Alvin Plantinga to Alister McGrath, Dallas Willard to William Lane Craig, Francis Collins to Ian Hutchinson, and Peter Kreeft to N. T. Wright, to name but a few. The point of this *tiny* listing is only to illustrate that there are many who have gone before or are still with us today who have lived out their specifically Christian faith with their minds fully engaged. To categorically dismiss Christians as unthinking or irrational ignores the historical record. There are many who take seriously Jesus' teaching that his followers are to apply all of their rational and creative powers in their relationships with God, as has been modeled by some of the greatest thinkers and creative personalities in human history.

It should be recognized that loving God with all one's mind does not equate to *understanding*. Anyone who would seek to learn about or know a God whose essential attributes are infinite and eternal will quickly reach the limits of his or her understanding. God's ways and thoughts are above our own (Isaiah 55:8–9), but that should not be an impediment to accepting and loving God with all our being, including our minds. You and I thoughtfully consider and accept many things that we do not understand, including in my case the physics of flying and the benefit of a prescribed medication. Yet I risk my very life by embracing these on a regular basis. One might object that *others* understand these things even while I do not, but we could readily move to other examples such as the faithful love of a friend, or the evocative quality of music, art, or poetry, to see that all of us experience, love, accept, and *act upon* things that we do not fully understand.

Applying our strength in loving God goes well beyond just our physical bodies and abilities and also includes all the other temporal resources we have. This is illustrated in Jesus' various stories about the importance of how people use their monies, talents, time, and opportunities. We learn that everything ultimately belongs to God; we are but stewards of the resources we have and are accountable to Him for how we use them. Therefore, we are to express our love for God by using whatever resources we have in ways consistent with His purposes.

The church has at times appeared overly focused on sexual purity as the sum total of scriptural teaching regarding our bodies. Indeed, notwithstanding the high-esteem accorded David, Abraham and the

Patriarchs, many of whom had multiple sexual partners, the scriptures *do* encourage sexual purity and marital fidelity (Psalm 119:9; Hebrews 13:4). Jesus himself, while extending grace to the woman caught in adultery, encouraged her to "go and sin no more" (John 8:11). Nevertheless, he had more to say about using one's physical strength and resources for good to bless others than he ever did about our sexuality (Mark 9:41; Matthew 5:16, 6:1–4). Jesus' emphasis always seemed to be on doing what we can and using whatever we have, no matter how much or little, to show genuine love of God through tangible service to others.

In responding to the lawyer's question that loving God above all else and with all that we are and have is the greatest commandment, Jesus was not proclaiming an unrealistic standard that will quickly crush us under the weight of its yoke. Instead, he was essentially teaching us that even as flawed and imperfect people, with all our failures and weaknesses, there is no sphere of our human experiences in which we can be unconcerned with honoring God, or effectively say, "I've got this—I don't need you." There is no aspect of my life that is off-limits to God. My commitment to live God's way cannot be confined to my church life or family life. I must dispel the notion that there are secular parts of my life in which God has no say. In my work life, social life, entertainment choices, thought life, computer usage, school life, dating, sex life, marriage, parenting, and finances, my pursuit of God always matters. While not attaining perfection, a follower of Christ will consider God in all that he or she does. That is of first importance and the key to living Jesus' way.

> ***Principle 1: Love God above all else—***
> ***consider Him in all that you do.***

CHAPTER 3

Loving Others

Don't surround yourself with yourself
—Yes

I first learned of the story of *Les Misérables* as a teenager, while watching the 1978 British made-for-TV-movie version of Victor Hugo's nineteenth-century masterpiece. Even then, I was deeply moved by the life-changing gesture of the kindly bishop Myriel to Jean Valjean. As you may recall, after Myriel took the escaped convict Valjean in when no one else would, Valjean "repaid" his kindness by stealing the bishop's silver and fleeing. When later apprehended, Valjean was brought back to the bishop by the police, who were understandably suspicious about the silver in Valjean's knapsack. The bishop, however, surprised everyone by telling the police that the silver was a gift to Valjean and then presented him with two more silver candlesticks, saying he had forgotten to take them when he left. After the police departed, Bishop Myriel privately encouraged Valjean to use the silver to become an honest man, and Valjean left, determined to be the man the bishop believed he could be. He and his life course were forever changed by this radical, loving act.

In his song "The Power of Love", T-Bone Burnett wrote that "the power of love can make a gangster cry, can make a loser try." That was certainly true for Jean Valjean, and probably for many of us as well. Love's awesome power has been recognized throughout the ages. The ancient Greek playwright Sophocles observed nearly twenty-five hundred years ago, "One word frees us of all the weight and pain of life: that word is love." And if we have lived with our eyes open, we have seen that love is utterly unlike anything else in the human experience for, as Dr. Martin Luther King Jr. powerfully preached, "Love is the only force capable of turning an enemy into a friend" (King 1957). Such is the power of love.

After telling the inquiring lawyer that the foremost principle of life is to love God with all we have and are, and above all else, Jesus added a second principle that cannot be separated from the first. "And the second is like it: 'Love your neighbor as yourself'" (Matthew 22:39).

Jesus explained that all the Law and the Prophets hang on these two commandments (Matthew 22:40). His earliest followers understood the application to their words and their lives:

> Whoever claims to love God yet hates a brother or sister is a liar. For whoever does not love their brother and sister, whom they have seen, cannot love God, whom they have not seen. (1 John 4:20)

Jesus' whole life and ministry demonstrated this fundamental point: loving God includes loving other people. In fact, he taught that the identifying mark of his true followers is their love for others (John 13:35). The failure to love others, even the most marginalized, disenfranchised and needy among us, in tangible ways when the opportunity presents itself, is an indication that our faith is not genuine and we do not really love God, no matter what our words say (Matthew 25:44). The necessary tie between authentic faith and love for others is so fundamental that it led the apostle Paul to observe, "The only thing that counts is faith expressing itself through love" (Galatians 5:6). Without love, talk of our faith is just worthless noise (1 Corinthians 13:1).

You and I reference love in imprecise ways, speaking perhaps of our undying love for our mates, love of God, and loving the beach, golf, puppies, and chocolate chip cookies in the same conversation. But the Greek word *agape* used in various forms in the New Testament where we find Jesus' teachings does not lend itself to such multiple meanings. It is a different concept in Greek than *philia,* describing friendship or brotherly love; *storge,* describing natural affection; or *eros,* describing intense or sexual desire. In appropriate contexts, such relational experiences are good and highly valued. Nevertheless, they do not capture the meaning of Christ's teaching regarding the love for others that is fundamental to living his way.

Jesus gave our *neighbor,* not some faceless, nameless grouping of others, as his primary example of those we are to love. But who, then, is my neighbor? Jesus told us, of course, starting with his parable of the good Samaritan who showed mercy and tended to the needs of the beaten and robbed man left in his path (Luke 10:25–37). The Samaritan's love was not abstract, and it undoubtedly resulted in him getting bloodied and dirty, not to mention costing him time and money. We see immediately in Jesus' illustration that we cannot be content to love at a distance but must be engaged with others around us in all of the messy inconvenience and sacrifice that that may involve.

It would be easy to generalize our love for others, even the least of people, such as the desperately poor in Haiti or the homeless in our communities, as a rationalization for keeping a comfortable spot on the sidelines. However, Jesus' words and example will not allow for that. My love must be shown to the person right here and now, like the beaten man left on the road travelled by the Samaritan. That is not to suggest that Christ-followers should not love or serve those who have no place to live, or the needy in Haiti, or unknown people on the other side of the world, but may we not do so as a means of avoiding *real engagement* with the individuals who are in our paths or right next door.

At the end of his story, Jesus turned the question on his listeners and asked which of the three characters who encountered the man in need *proved to be his neighbor?* The question is loaded because the beaten man was Jewish, like Jesus' audience and the priest and Levite who refused to help, and he did not—would not—live next door to a despised Samaritan. The answer was obvious, but the lawyer who responded could not even bring himself to utter the word "Samaritan" in a positive light, instead replying, "The one who had mercy on him" (Luke 10:37). We would miss a central point in Jesus' deliberate juxtaposition of the Samaritan and the Jewish man he helped if we failed to recognize that their racial and religious divide was deep, long-standing and intense, leaving little, if any, chance that either felt affection for the other.

We thus learn that this love to which Jesus' followers are called does not necessarily involve an emotional feeling, but rather a choice to seek

17

the good of the one loved. At its essence, such love means that we are to *act in the interest of the other,* regardless of our feelings. Jesus thereby distinguished our common conception of love as emotion or feeling by illustrating that *agape* is volitional, not emotional. It is fundamentally a choice of our will. If we are to be followers of Christ, then, we must love others whether or not we feel like it.

Jesus further explained his call to love by proclaiming that it applies even if the other person does not love you back:

> If you love those who love you, what credit is that to you? Even sinners love those who love them. And if you do good to those who are good to you, what credit is that to you? Even sinners do that. (Luke 6:32–33)

In fact, Jesus taught that we must go beyond those who seek our good, or are indifferent to us, and also love our enemies, who, by definition, are those who would seek to *harm* us:

> But love your enemies, do good to them, and lend to them without expecting to get anything back. Then your reward will be great, and you will be children of the Most High, because he is kind to the ungrateful and wicked. Be merciful, just as your Father is merciful. (Luke 6:35–36)

What are we to make of a love that is to be shown to those who refuse or fail to love us back, and even to those who wish or seek our harm? *Agape* is not only volitional (instead of emotional), but also it is unconditional. It therefore follows that the scope of Jesus' command to love is not limited to the family of like-minded people or fellow believers—it includes all people. There is *no one* who is beyond our mandate to love. We are to seek the good of all others, whether or not they love us back and even if they wish to harm us.

It is obvious that such love for others may be costly. Instead of glossing over that fact, Jesus emphasizes it, teaching us that great love involves great sacrifice:

> My command is this: Love each other as I have loved
> you. Greater love has no one than this: to lay down one's
> life for one's friends. You are my friends if you do what I
> command. (John 15:12–14)

In fact, it is Jesus' own example that drives home his teaching about love: "This is how we know what love is: Jesus Christ laid down his life for us. And we ought to lay down our lives for our brothers and sisters" (1 John 3:16). Whether "laying down our lives" in love for others proves to be literal or figurative in one's own experience, it is clear that in addition to being volitional and unconditional, *agape* is also sacrificial.

Jesus does not give the reasons in his story of the good Samaritan as to why the religious people passed by without helping the ailing man, but he invites us to fill in those blanks from our own experiences: "I don't have the time," "I'll get dirty," "I'll be late to my meeting," "I can't afford to help," etc. Whatever reason I might give for not stopping to help the man, it is clear that *my focus is on me* and *not* the man who needs help. By contrast, the Samaritan's focus is undoubtedly on the injured man and his needs, not only in the immediate term but also in the long-term, as well.

As a master teacher, Jesus explains his categorical call to love others so as to preempt our natural objections: What if I do not feel like it? What if the person does not love me back? What if it costs me? His command is clear—we are to love anyway. But *how*, we might ask, how do I love someone like that? We do so by regarding the interests and needs of others as we do our own. In Jesus' words: "So in everything, do to others what you would have them do to you, for this sums up the Law and the Prophets" (Matthew 7:12). Jesus' teaching and example also demonstrate that this Golden Rule of loving others is characterized in service to them (Mark 9:35).

Even when we are called to love someone who we really *do not like*, we may *act* like it. If we are to seek the good of another whether or not we feel like it, and whether or not they love us back, what other conclusion could there be? But, as a friend once protested to me, isn't that hypocritical? To the contrary, choosing to seek the good of another even when I do not feel like it or they do not do the same in return is a true *selfless act*, and applies the perspective that Jesus calls his followers to have. Hypocrisy is saying or doing one thing while intending another. It is hypocritical for me to pretend that I am seeking your good when I am really trying to get something from you. But when my motive is to seek your good, in spite of my own feelings, and whether you can or will do something for me in return, then I am capturing the essence of Christ's command to love my neighbor as myself.

Someone who feels little self-love might be struck by Jesus' reference to self and object that it would be wrong to love others according to that standard. But such a self-assessment is again grounded in the concept of love as a feeling, and if we instead see love as Jesus taught—essentially seeking the good of another irrespective of our feelings or whether they love us back—then we will see that Jesus was not giving a qualification that presumed his followers had a good self-image. Rather, he was recognizing the truism that *all* of us naturally look out for our own interests. That is, seeking our own good is our inherent bent—our default positions, if you will. Now, we may be deluded as to what is good for us, not unlike an addict who is convinced that he or she should have another hit of heroin. Even then, however, we are acting upon our tendency to pursue what we have convinced ourselves is good for us.

It would be difficult for any of us to honestly observe life—our own or the lives around us—without seeing that the choices people make are typically motivated out of self-interest. Although this reality about human nature fuels our American economic and political systems, is deftly played by the advertisers of Madison Avenue, and can certainly be positively and productively channeled, it creates problems when self-interest is pursued above all else and irrespective of the consequences to others. Try an experiment sometime. Review your typical news source for one week, whether Internet, TV, radio, social media, or newspaper. As you consider the reports of calamity, dysfunction, and man's inhumanity toward his fellow man, ask yourself whether one or more of the people in the story is elevating his or her interests above another's. On a fundamental level, you will see that is always the case. The empirical evidence is simply overwhelming that humans have a natural bent toward self-centeredness.

Such evidence has not escaped the notice of the poets of our age. In his song "License to Kill," Bob Dylan wrote of mankind,

> Now he worships at an altar by a stagnant pool, and when
> he sees his reflection, he's fulfilled. Man is opposed to fair
> play. He wants it all and he wants it his way.

This may seem like a harsh indictment of us all, but the scriptures confirm that the desire to have our own way—selfish ambition—is both the cause and the lasting consequence of our sinfulness and every evil practice (Genesis 3:2–7; James 3:16). As the prophet Isaiah wrote, "We all, like sheep, have gone astray, each of us has turned to our own way" (Isaiah 53:6).

According to Jesus, we were not created to elevate our own interests above our neighbor's. In fact, Jesus came and died, according to the scriptures, so that we do not have to live self-centered lives any longer: "And he died for all, that those who live should no longer live for themselves but for him who died for them and was raised again" (2 Corinthians 5:15). The apostle Paul recognized that a practical way to guard against our natural self-centeredness is to have the same mindset as Jesus: "In humility, value others above yourselves, not looking to your own interests, but each of you to the interests of the others" (Philippians 2:3–5). Instead of only focusing on our own needs and wants, Jesus called us to show similar regard for the interests of others.

In explaining that we were made to love God with all our beings and above all else, and to love others as ourselves, Jesus offered the truth that sets us free from our self-centered condition:

> Jesus said, "If you hold to my teaching, you are really my
> disciples. Then you will know the truth, and the truth will
> set you free... So if the Son sets you free, you will be free
> indeed. (John 8:31–36)

And that liberation, his early followers understood, frees us to serve one another humbly in love (Galatians 5:13). Instead of embracing self-interest as our prime value, Jesus shared that we should regard the interests of other people as thoughtfully as we do our own. This is true even when we do not feel like it, when it is costly, and when we receive nothing in return.

Principle 2: Love others—seek their good, whether or not you feel like it or they do the same, and even if it costs you.

CHAPTER 4

Forgiving Others

You better put it all behind you; 'cause life goes on.
If you keep carrying that anger, it will eat you up inside baby.
—Don Henley

A horrible tragedy occurred in Nickel Mines, Pennsylvania, on October 2, 2006, when a disturbed gunman stormed a schoolhouse filled with Amish children. After driving all the boys and teachers out, he bound the ten remaining young girls and systematically shot them before turning the gun on himself. By the time his siege ended, five young girls lay dead, and five others were critically wounded. The crime was shocking in its cruelty and audacity, and stands out even as school shootings in America continue at a nauseating pace. What is most memorable to me, however, is the image of the Amish friends and family of the children who were shot, reaching out within hours to the family of the shooter, extending their forgiveness for his unspeakable acts and checking on his family's well-being. Such grace is as irrepressible as it is unexpected, and bleeds through the darkness of that day, continuing even now in the changed lives and witness of the shooter's widow and mother, among others.

There was a time when the question "What Would Jesus Do?" was everywhere, with people often putting the inquiry to themselves (or others) by wearing plastic bracelets with the initials WWJD. The question may be provocative and the answer nuanced or unclear at times, but *not* when it comes to suffering wrong at the hands of another. Jesus would forgive. It would be impossible to rationally understand his teachings and example any other way. With his dying breath, Jesus even extended forgiveness to his executioners (Luke 23:34). Teaching his followers to forgive others, and what that means, was central to Jesus' ministry.

While the categorical nature of Jesus' instruction on forgiveness is startling enough, he really grabs our attention with the tie-in to our own forgiveness by God:

> For if you forgive men when they sin against you, your heavenly Father will also forgive you. But if you do not forgive men their sins, your Father will not forgive your sins. (Matthew 6:14–15)

This explanation follows the Lord's Prayer in which we pray that God "forgive us our trespasses, as we forgive our trespassers," so there is little chance that we misunderstand those familiar words. In the famous story of the ungrateful servant who was shown forgiveness of a great debt by his creditor but refused to extend forgiveness of a comparably small debt to his own debtor (Matthew 18:23–35), Jesus underscores the connection between God's forgiveness and our own. While that connection may be somewhat mysterious in a theological sense, there is no denying that Jesus was very, very serious about his mandate that we forgive.

Jesus explained that forgiveness means we are not to track or keep score of the offenses committed against us:

> Then Peter came to Jesus and asked, "Lord, how many times shall I forgive my brother when he sins against me? Up to seven times?" Jesus answered, "I tell you, not seven times, but seventy-seven times." (Matthew 18: 21–22)

We may not dwell on or obsess over the wrongs inflicted on us by another, no matter how egregious or frequent they might be.

We are also not to seek revenge or try to get back at the wrongdoer:

> You have heard that it was said, "Eye for eye, and tooth for tooth." But I tell you, do not resist an evil person. If anyone slaps you on the right cheek, turn to them the other cheek also. And if anyone wants to sue you and take your shirt, hand over your coat as well. (Matthew 5: 38–40)

The payback or settling of scores has no place in the life of a Christ-follower. This core instruction was understood by Jesus' earliest followers, who were told, "Do not take revenge" (Romans 12:19), and encouraged to "forgive one another if any of you has a grievance against someone. Forgive as the Lord forgave you" (Colossians 3:13).

So, if we are not to keep track of others' offenses or try to pay them back, but instead are to love and pray for them, and forgive them as God has forgiven us, what is the essential quality of forgiveness as taught by Jesus? It is that we do not hold the wrongs of others against them. Jesus confirmed that when he said, "[And] when you stand praying, if you hold anything against anyone, forgive them" (Mark 11:25).

Focusing on that essential nature of forgiveness also helps us to understand what it is *not*. For starters, forgiveness is not the same as *excusing* another's behavior. As eloquently discussed by C. S. Lewis in his "Essay on Forgiveness," when we excuse another's actions, we are saying that they could not help it or did not mean it, so they are really not to blame. When we forgive, however, we acknowledge the wrong in all its intended hurtfulness, recognize it as inexcusable, and yet choose never to hold it against the wrongdoer so that everything between us will be as it was before (Lewis 1960, 2). Lewis sums up his observation by recognizing the double standard into which we often lapse, and contrasts our calling as followers of Christ:

> In our own case we accept excuses too easily; in other people's we do not accept them easily enough… To excuse what can really produce good excuses is not Christian charity; it is only fairness. To be a Christian means to forgive the inexcusable, because God has forgiven the inexcusable in you. (ibid.)

We may have heard, or even said ourselves, "I will forgive, but never forget." If we never forget, it sounds the same as holding the sin against the person. While that may be at times what we really mean, it may not always be. Some offenses are just so terrible that we constantly live with the consequences of them. To hope to forget them would be folly. We are urged to forgive, however, even though we may be confronted with reminders or the scar of the offense every day of our lives. The essence of forgiveness is to not hold the wrong which we may well-remember against the wrongdoer. In fact, as Paul Tillich observed, we often must *remember in order* to forgive:

> Forgiving presupposes remembering. And it creates a forgetting not in the natural way we forget yesterday's weather, but in the way of the great "in spite of" that says: I forget although I remember… I speak of the lasting willingness to accept him who has hurt us. (Tillich 1963, 23)

It also follows, then, that forgiving even a single offense of another person may take many times. Every time we remember how the person wronged us, as often as it comes to our mind, we are presented with the choice to forgive or not. That fits as much into Jesus' admonition to Peter as does not keeping score. When seen this way, our remembrance of a person's wrong becomes not an obstacle to forgiveness, but rather another opportunity to extend it.

If we set aside for a moment the clarity of Jesus' instruction that we forgive others, we might ask *why* we should do so, especially in the case of someone who has wronged us *egregiously*, and not in some trifling manner. Indeed, "Why Forgive?" is the question emblazoned on the cover of the 1984 *Time* magazine depicting Pope John Paul II extending forgiveness to Mehmet Ali Agca, who shot him four times in a failed assassination attempt (Morrow 1984). Initially, we cannot overlook that forgiving another is *the loving thing to do*. It is treating the wrongdoer the way we would want to be treated, which at its root is the practical application of our mandate to love others, even our enemies (Matthew 5:44). Frankly, it would be difficult to conceive of a more pure form of love in action than choosing not to hold another's wrong against him or her.

But forgiving others is also for our own sakes. If I do not forgive, I will necessarily harbor resentment that eventually will rob me of my own joy and leave me bitter. Therefore, *my* life is diminished by my refusal to forgive another. Many of us need look no further than our own life experiences to realize that is true. Others, like Edith Shoals, whose eighteen-year-old daughter, Lordette, was shot and killed while talking with her mother on the phone, realize this truth in nearly unfathomable circumstances: "Grieving's not a big enough word for what happens. But if you don't forgive, it eats you up from the inside out" (Linn 2015). As difficult as it may be to apply, following Jesus' instruction to forgive spares us the bitterness that refusing to do so produces.

Forgiveness also keeps us from being stuck in an unending cycle of pay back and retribution. As author Philip Yancey observed,

> Vengeance is a passion to get even. It is a hot desire to give back as much pain as someone gives you. The problem with revenge is that it never gets what it wants; it never evens the score. Fairness never comes. The chain reaction set off by every act of vengeance always takes its unhindered course. It ties both the injured and the injurer to an escalator of pain. Both are stuck on the escalator as long as parity is demanded, and the escalator never stops, never lets anyone off" … Forgiveness ALONE can break the cycle of blame and pain, breaking the chain of ungrace. (Yancey 1997, 96)

The pursuit of revenge keeps us enslaved, but the truth of forgiveness sets us free. To *not* forgive locks us in the past and also locks us out of all potential for change. Forgiveness is the key which unlocks those chains.

For that practical reason, we cannot wait for another to repent or apologize before we extend forgiveness. If we wait to forgive, we will have effectively given that person the ability to rob or qualify our joy, leaving us to essentially live our own lives with an asterisk (*). In the most extreme reaction, when we are wholly committed to exact revenge, we will have ceded *control* of our lives to the other. That is because our decisions cue off the other person's actions—his or her moves dictate our moves.

Occasionally Christians point to some of Jesus' words to suggest that our forgiveness of others is dependent on them first repenting of their wrong against us: "If your brother or sister sins against you, rebuke them; and if they repent, forgive them" (Luke 17:3). But interpreting this partial passage so narrowly overlooks Jesus' own example at the cross with his executioners. "Father, forgive them," he prayed, even though they continued to carry out their grim task without any apparent repentance or acknowledgement of the injustice they were causing. And how could such an interpretation be reconciled with Jesus' tie between our willingness to forgive others and our own forgiveness? "Forgive, and you will be forgiven," he said (Luke 6:37). With respect to our own wrongdoing, would we really risk forgiveness by God, or even another person, because of our insistence that those who have wronged us first demonstrate repentance or apologize before we extend our forgiveness?

More practically, withholding our forgiveness unless the wrongdoer first repents or apologizes ignores the fact that he or she may *never* apologize or seek our forgiveness. That realistic possibility exposes why it is foolish to impose a condition on our willingness to forgive. For one thing, the other person may not even be aware of the wrong, perhaps because of insensitivity or because the offense was an unintended slight that we have blown out of proportion. We may thus be stewing while the other person goes about his or her life, oblivious to our hurt and anger. Even if that is not the case, and the offense was very great and intentional, our insistence on an apology before we let go of our anger and forgive merely provides another weapon for the wrongdoer to continue to inflict emotional wounds on us and disrupt our lives, essentially giving him or her another victim.

Christ-followers must take the initiative when it comes to forgiveness, just like the scriptures teach that God did with us (1 John 4:19). We must be willing to make the first move. It would be difficult to imagine any scenario in which we could be more Christ-like than when we extend forgiveness to one who has deliberately wronged us and neither acknowledges nor apologizes for it. With a new perspective, we may even consider the moments when we are wronged by others as the best chances we will have in this life to be like Jesus.

One difficulty with forgiveness is it seems *unfair*. But that is what makes it forgiveness. If the act is wrong, then the fair thing to do would be to make the person apologize or pay for the wrong he or she has committed. But forgiveness takes that compulsion out of the mix. Whether restitution is made may help achieve *justice*, but that is not a prerequisite to forgiveness. While justice is important in its own right, the issue with forgiveness—whether I will hold this wrong against the wrongdoer or not—remains even if restitution is never made or attempted.

It should be remembered that Jesus' instruction to forgive is directed toward us as individuals. It is not a prescription for how the state is to respond to the crimes of another. The purpose of the state includes the punishment of wrongdoers (1 Peter 2:14), and nowhere does Jesus suggest otherwise. What the state does in fulfilling its function, however, has nothing to do with our individual mandate to forgive. We may still choose to not hold the wrong of another against him or her even as the state prosecutes that person to the full extent of the law.

Forgiveness is Jesus' way. It is hard for us and not necessarily instantaneous. It will often take time as we process and grieve the hurt caused by another. Perhaps that process is helped by following Jesus' teaching to *pray* for those who hurt us (Matthew 5:44), as it is difficult for me to dwell on a hurt or hold a grudge against one for whom I am genuinely praying. There may also never be an opportunity or desire to be in the presence of the one who may have wronged me so terribly, but I can still refuse to hold his wrong against him, wish him well—even if only in my mind's eye—*and mean it*. And, if contact with the other person is unavoidable, the issue will not be the emotions I may or may not feel, but rather how I act toward that person in spite of his or her wrong. If I am a Christ-follower, the choice is clear—I must forgive.

Principle 3: Forgive others—don't hold their wrongs against them.

CHAPTER 5

Judging Others

Don't you look at me so smug, and say I'm going bad.
Who are you to judge me and the life that I live?
—Bob Marley

If you were to poll a group of people who have heard of Jesus but want nothing to do with him or a church that bears his name, chances are they would say that Christian churches are full of judgmental, self-righteous hypocrites. This criticism has some merit as the church is comprised of flawed people like you and me who often do not practice what we preach, and there is no doubt that collectively the church can be more vocal about what it is against than its invitation to the weary and heavy-laden to hear and receive the good news of the gospel. We seem determined to point out to nonbelievers the ways in which they are wrong, when Jesus' approach was to talk and eat with them, and let them know they did not have to run or hide any longer because their sins could be forgiven. The reason Jesus came, he explained, was to find and save people who had lost their way (Luke 19:10). Maybe people who were not church-going loved to spend time with Jesus, and not so much us, because people react differently to being found than they do to being judged.

The irony of Christians judging other people in the name of Christ is that Jesus said repeatedly *he* did not come to judge the world:

> If anyone hears my words but does not keep them, I do not judge that person. For I did not come to judge the world, but to save the world. (John 12:47)

> For God did not send the Son into the world to judge the
> world, but that the world should be saved through Him.
> (John 3:17 NASB)

More ironic still is that Jesus told his followers to *not* judge others:

> Do not judge, or you too will be judged. For in the same way
> you judge others, you will be judged, and with the measure
> you use, it will be measured to you. (Matthew 7:1-2)

Although Jesus' first followers, like us, also struggled with being judgmental at times, they were reminded that this was contrary to Jesus' teachings and example. The principle given throughout the New Testament is that each of us should recognize God is the true judge, and everyone will one day give an account to God for his or her own life:

> You, then, why do you judge your brother or sister? Or
> why do you treat them with contempt? For we will all
> stand before God's judgment seat. (Romans 14:10)

> Therefore judge nothing before the appointed time; wait
> until the Lord comes. He will bring to light what is hidden
> in darkness and will expose the motives of the heart.
> At that time each will receive their praise from God. (1
> Corinthians 4:5)

While Jesus' command that we not judge others is clear, he does not resort to "because I said so" as the reason we should live by his teaching. Instead, he points to a deeper truth that explains how it is in our best interests to live the way he showed and taught us. By judging other people, he says, we are setting ourselves up for judgment.

To explore the full impact of this principle, it is necessary to consider what Jesus means by "judging others." It should be obvious that life cannot be lived without making a series of judgments every day, and there are some who by position have a civic duty to pronounce formal judgments. But in telling us to not judge others, Jesus is not talking about discernment or making choices based on our assessment of a situation or person, nor is he referring to the judicial decisions handed down in a legal system. Neither is the person who accuses Christians of being judgmental.

What Jesus and the critic are referring to specifically is the tendency to focus on and point out faults in other people. And why do we do that? We point to their faults—whether wrongs they have committed, mistakes they have made, or physical or character flaws they have—*in order to make them look bad.* And the reason we try to make others look bad is so that we look better by comparison. In essence, we are telling whoever is listening (and ourselves) why we should be preferred, approved, or accepted over the others. We are saying, "We're better than them."

But what about relationships in which we have a responsibility to correct the behavior or attitude of another person, such as we might have at times with family members, employees or a teacher to student? I heard a man share his story recently, and he relayed how poorly he had treated his girlfriend when they were in college together. When his partying and promiscuous lifestyle led him to rock bottom and he decided that he wanted to change his course, he reached out to his by now ex-girlfriend's father for help because he did not know where else to turn.

Instead of condemning him for his behavior, her father encouraged him with this message: "You're better than that." That proved life changing for this man, and besides breaking free of his destructive lifestyle, he ultimately married the young lady, and now works in his father-in-law's firm.

This man's testimony illustrates an important distinction between judging another person and providing correction in appropriate contexts. When we judge another, we are pointing out his or her faults to make them look bad. When we correct someone, on the other hand, the sincere desire is for him or her to become better. We are seeking their good and helping where we have been given opportunity. Can the other person misperceive our motives in specific instances of constructive criticism or correction? Sure, just as we can be less than forthright about intending our comments for their betterment. If we are honest, we will see that people are pretty adept at recognizing when we are communicating in words or deeds a message that they are inferior to us.

If our approach with other people is to criticize them and call attention to their mistakes or struggles in order to make them look bad, Jesus says they will approach us the same way; that is, they will use "the same measure." One need only reflect on some well-publicized examples to see that this is so. People love to turn our own words against us, so it was with great glee that the public condemned and mocked a well-known TV preacher for his sexual encounters with a prostitute because he was so vocal in his condemnation of "the world's" sexual practices.

After a particular pastor of a large church spoke out loudly against homosexuality, the criticism from the public was deafening and it was regarded as "national news" when his own sexual experiences with another man came to light.

Think also about the politics of the workplace and how coworkers respond to an employee who always seems to have something bad to say about another. Criticism and scorn will rain down when that bad-mouthing employee messes up. Jesus reminds us that is how it works. What goes around comes around. The standard we use will be used against us, and often with great relish.

The self-defeating nature of being judgmental is underscored when we acknowledge that the reason we call attention to the faults of others is ultimately to make them look bad, and us better by comparison, so that we win approval or acceptance. But if other people sense our judgmental spirit and air of superiority (and they almost always will), they will look for opportunities to turn the tables on us and urge our rejection by others. Thus, the strategic intention in our approach is undermined because of it.

Another reason that we must not judge goes to Jesus' earlier commands that his followers love and forgive other people. How can we sincerely love or forgive them when we are focused on pointing out their faults and trying to make them look bad? We cannot. Saying or thinking that we are better than others, and loving and forgiving them, are mutually exclusive concepts. Thus, if we who claim to be Christ-followers are unconcerned about displaying a judgmental attitude toward a person or group of people, not only are we acting contrary to Jesus' command to not judge others, but also we are unable to show them the love and forgiveness that are fundamental to living Jesus' way. That is no small thing in the context of Jesus' words that his true followers are not those who merely call him "Lord, Lord," but rather those who do what he says.

The seriousness of this disconnect between Jesus' teachings and a judgmental attitude or spirit is further underscored by our earlier observation that many people want nothing to do with Christ's church because they perceive—often accurately—that Christians are "so judgmental." Thus, when Jesus' so-called followers make it their business to judge others, they are effectively *driving others away* from him, which is diametrically opposed to the Great Commission that Jesus gave his followers to go into all the world and make disciples. We should remember Jesus' words:

> Whoever is not with me is against me; and whoever does
> not gather with me, scatters. (Luke 11:23)

The sobering reminder is that being judgmental of others—pointing out their faults in order to cast them in a negative light—not only prevents us from following Jesus' teachings, it pits us *against him*.

Instead of focusing on the faults of others, Jesus calls his followers to address their own:

> Why do you look at the speck of sawdust in your brother's
> eye and pay no attention to the plank in your own eye?
> How can you say to your brother, 'Let me take the speck
> out of your eye,' when all the time there is a plank in your
> own eye? You hypocrite, first take the plank out of your
> own eye, and then you will see clearly to remove the speck
> from your brother's eye. (Matthew 7:3–5)

When I see a fault in you or another, my response must not be to point it out, and convey that "I think I am better than you." Rather, I must examine my own self to see if that fault is also in me (or work on it if I already know it is). Such an approach preempts any rational charge of self-righteous condemnation and instead displays a humility that is undeniably Christ-like and, more often than not, winsome. It is also liberating. I will not waste my time and energy trying to make others look bad and myself better by comparison. Instead, I am set free to love them unconditionally, flaws and all, just as Jesus said his followers should, and the way he said God loves us all.

Principle 4: Instead of judging others and focusing on their faults, address your own.

CHAPTER 6

Showing Off

You had one eye in the mirror as you watched yourself gavotte
—Carly Simon

From time to time I meet someone who struggles with sibling rivalry. The kind I am referring to is not merely heightened competition in the classroom or on the ball field, but a rivalry borne of a deep-seated conviction, perhaps with good reason, that one's brother or sister was blatantly favored by their parents and teachers. And, while the one's every move was criticized, the favored sibling could do no wrong. If unchecked, such situations can lead to pathological feelings of inadequacy in the one constantly trying to measure up. The unending comparisons—"Why can't you just be more like your brother?"—will result in bitterness and resentment that can be a burden carried for a lifetime.

I know a middle-aged woman who struggles to this day with the perception that her sister was always "Little Miss Perfect," sweetly gliding down the straight and narrow path under the approving gaze of Mom, Dad, and a throng of admirers, in contrast to her own journey which was more meandering and punctuated by considerable time "in the ditch."

Even outside the family context, we have a tendency as people to compare ourselves to others and make conclusions about how bad or good we are. You know the drill. When confronted with our own mistakes or shortcomings, we may say or think, "At least I'm not as bad as Ted Bundy," or Jack the Ripper, or some other notorious person. And most of us probably know the feeling when we have poured ourselves into a project—whether in school or our jobs—and felt pretty good about it until we saw the extraordinary project turned in by our classmate or coworker. The worst part is when we catch that look of superiority from them after the grade, award, or promotion is announced and come to the realization that they *really might* be better than you or me!

The men and women who gathered to hear Jesus teach his famed Sermon on the Mount must have felt a chill run down their collective spines when he said:

> For I tell you that unless your righteousness surpasses
> that of the Pharisees and the teachers of the law, you will
> certainly not enter the kingdom of heaven. (Matthew 5:20)

To that Jewish audience, the Pharisees and teachers of the law were the very definition of righteousness. They were holy men who were both feared and held by the people in high esteem. Many had memorized and could recite the Torah, telling listeners the middle word, even the middle *letter*, of the entire scriptures. To say they were "holier than thou" was an understatement, and probably a cause of some resentment among the people. The burden or yoke they put on the people in terms of religious and moral requirements was heavy and oppressive. The standard of righteousness they portrayed would have been considered by the people as a bar too high and beyond their reach.

So what did Jesus mean in telling the crowd that they had no chance unless their righteousness topped the righteousness of those ultrareligious guys? We get some insight into what characterizes the "righteousness of the Pharisees" in these words of Christ:

> The teachers of the law and the Pharisees sit in Moses' seat.
> So you must be careful to do everything they tell you. But
> do not do what they do, for they do not practice what they
> preach. They tie up heavy, cumbersome loads and put
> them on other people's shoulders, but they themselves are
> not willing to lift a finger to move them. "Everything they
> do is done for people to see… those who exalt themselves
> will be humbled, and those who humble themselves will
> be exalted. (Matthew 23:2–12)

The Pharisees and teachers of the law exalted themselves, and doing so was their full-time occupation. Jesus repeatedly called them on this, and pointed out that theirs was not true righteousness, but rather a *self-righteous* show. In telling his listeners that their righteousness must exceed that of those religious leaders, Jesus was saying that we must *not* be self-righteous, for self-righteous people have no place in God's kingdom. It is not those who exalt themselves in pride, but rather those who are humble who receive God's blessing, for "God is opposed to the proud, but gives grace to the humble" (James 4:6 NASB).

While that alone should be sufficient warning to make us flee from the Pharisees' approach, there are other good reasons to avoid self-righteousness. For one thing, it is a phony act, because calling attention to our own good or religious deeds is fundamentally about how we *appear* and not how we really are. And like the Pharisees who did not practice what they preached, we will inevitably fail to attain even our own contrived standards (which we nonetheless seek to impose on others), and such hypocrisy will eventually be exposed, to our lasting shame. Additionally, Jesus' strongest recorded words were spoken against these people who pridefully viewed themselves as righteous (Matthew 23:13–33). In fact, his indictments of them were so scathing that they decided they would kill him in order to shut him up. If we want to be Jesus' followers, why would we act like them?

To sidestep the trap of self-righteousness, Jesus instructed his followers to avoid doing their deeds of righteousness in order to be seen by others. In fact, in contrast to the religious show-offs, we are to be intentional in *not* calling attention to our religious acts and good deeds. He used specific examples that go to the heart of the approach of the Pharisees and self-righteous, religious people everywhere, including praying, fasting, and giving to the needy while calling attention to themselves (Matthew 6:1–6, 16–18). Jesus observes that doing such things in order to impress others provides no lasting satisfaction even if our "show" succeeds in garnering their praise. And, if we do our acts of "worship" or good deeds in order to be seen or recognized, Jesus tells us that we somehow *negate* any reward from God. In short, the praise or reward of men will be all there is, and as we know, even that is no sure thing.

Consider also that our religious acts of worship are those in which we recognize and honor God and His attributes. Praying, fasting, and giving certainly qualify, and by definition, such worship should be fundamentally directed toward God. But if we are, instead, performing such acts in order to be seen and impress others who may (or may not) be watching, it follows that our worship itself *cannot* be genuine. In fact, no matter how religious we try to make our acts seem, they are not worship at all but are instead merely grandstanding.

The irony, explains Jesus, is that God *is* watching us and is well-aware of our ulterior motives, so He sees through our charade even if others do not. Everyone else may fall for it or may not even care if I, for example, make that big donation to my church just to get my name on a building, but if Jesus' teaching is true, God sees through that. The prophet Samuel was reminded that God sees things differently than we do when Samuel was directed to anoint a king to succeed Saul:

> But the LORD said to Samuel, "Do not consider his appearance or his height, for I have rejected him. The LORD does not look at the things people look at. People look at the outward appearance, but the LORD looks at the heart." (1 Samuel 16:7)

In the same way, Jesus explains that God is aware of our righteous deeds that are sincerely motivated: "Your Father, who sees what is done in secret, will reward you" (Matthew 6:4). If that is true, and if there is a chance of us negating God's reward by calling attention to our deeds, we must not insist on recognition or affirmation from others. Nor should we fret when people ignore or overlook the good that we have done. While it may at times be very tempting to let people know, for example, that we are fasting or have given a donation to the church or those in need, Jesus teaches us to resist so as to guard against a self-righteous attitude creeping into our hearts.

The underlying truth is that God is the audience that matters, because He sees all that we do for what it truly is. Christian theologians have described this perspective in the Latin phrase *coram Deo,* literally "before the face of God," and have even insightfully recognized that this big idea extends beyond merely our worship and good deeds and applies to *all* aspects of life. Theologian and pastor R. C. Sproul writes,

> *Coram Deo* captures the essence of the Christian life. This phrase literally refers to something that takes place in the presence of, or before the face of, God… To live in the presence of God is to understand that whatever we are doing and wherever we are doing it, we are acting under the gaze of God… To live all of life *Coram Deo* is to live a life of integrity… that functions the same basic way in church and out of church. It is a life… in which all that is done is done as to the Lord. (Sproul 2015)

When we live this way, as Jesus reminds us, we find an audience of One who always knows whether our worship is genuine and our good deeds sincere, because God sees all and weighs our hearts.

There are immediate consequences to this change in perspective. For one thing, we are freed from the concern of being misunderstood. As a sign on the wall of Mother Teresa's children's home in Calcutta read, quoting *The Paradoxical Commandments,* "If you are kind, people may accuse you of selfish, ulterior motives. Be kind anyway" (Keith 2001). We can be assured that God will see our true intentions, even if others do not. Again, that is a two-edged sword as God will see our sincerity as well as our duplicity or mixed motives.

Living *coram Deo* also frees us from the need for affirmation by others. While it is certainly nice to be recognized, appreciated, or even thanked when we serve others, this is something that we cannot control and must not insist upon before we do for them the good that is within our power and opportunity to do. On one recorded occasion, Jesus healed ten lepers and only one, a Samaritan, had the good manners to say thanks (Luke 17:11–19). We all can probably recall acts of kindness we dispensed when the recipient not only did not thank us, but also acted as if he was *entitled* to our service. And let us be honest, when we do not get the thanks or recognition we think we deserve—or worse, it wrongly goes to another person—we are left resentful and embittered. Some of us have harbored such feelings for a long time, and they have thoroughly robbed our lives of joy. The antidote to such ills, says Jesus, is to look to God and not men and women for our recognition and reward.

The changed perspective of living our lives to please God instead of seeking the praise or recognition of men also frees us up to genuinely celebrate the accomplishments and good deeds of other people. We can congratulate them and *mean* it, without jealousy, resentment, or secretly wishing it was us who had done what they did. This approach would significantly impact almost everything we do, not only making us more winsome to others, but also filling our own lives with positivity and joy.

Some might recall that the Bible teaches we are created by God in Christ Jesus "to do good works which God prepared in advance for us to do" (Ephesians 2:10). And did not Jesus himself tell the people on the hill to "let your light shine before others, that they may see your good deeds and glorify your Father in heaven" (Matthew 5:16)?

As a practical matter, it would also seem nearly impossible to do all good deeds anonymously so that no one knows or notices who did them. The distinction Jesus makes, however, is concerning our motivation, that is, *why* we do the good deeds or acts of worship, which is well known to the "God who sees." If they are done to call attention to ourselves and show others how good and holy we are, then that is the essence of the righteousness of the Pharisees. If, however, our worship or good deeds are done so that others may recognize and experience God, then we have acted as Christ's followers, loving and serving those within our reach, even the least and marginalized, and working to bring God's kingdom "on earth, as it is in heaven."

If we dig deeper, we see that Jesus' principles of not judging others, and not showing off our religious or good deeds, are different sides of the same coin. Both are strategies intended to make ourselves look better. In one instance, we point out another's faults so that they look worse than us, and in the other instance, we point out our "righteousness" so that we look better than them. What is the common technique? *Comparing* ourselves to others, and we must avoid it, whether negative (when I focus on the faults of others) or positive (when I focus on my religious acts or good deeds). Either way, I am conveying the thought that I am better than someone else.

This tendency to compare myself to other people begs the question of why I am so committed to making myself look better than them, whether through being judgmental or exalting myself. Again, we do this to be accepted or approved. By whom? By others and ultimately, if we are people of faith, by God. This reveals something important about how we view the basis for a relationship with God, as it belies our perspective that we must win God's approval or convince him to accept us. It exposes our conviction that we can and must *do* something in order to be loved by God. Jesus, however, dispelled that notion in his very frank dialogue with a religious leader named Nicodemus by telling him,

> For God so loved the world that he gave his one and only Son, that whoever believes in him shall not perish but have eternal life. (John 3:16)

Jesus taught that God's love for all people is universal, emanating from God's nature and not our own worthiness. God's gracious invitation into His family and kingdom work is already there for anyone who wants it because of who Jesus is and what he did for us that we could not do for ourselves. That truth, said Jesus, is accepted by faith, not earned by anything we do, and is the start, or rebirth, of a new life. The outpouring of that faith in the form of a life committed to the good works and service that Jesus modeled and taught is inevitable, and essentially the family mark of his true followers. The good that we do is not the basis for our acceptance by God, but rather the result of it.

When we give in to the thinking that we must and can do enough to earn God's approval and acceptance, it shows that we do not really trust Jesus at his word, and we fall into the perspective of the older brother in Jesus' famous story of two sons (Luke 15:11–31). Upon seeing the loving, celebratory acceptance of his prodigal brother by their father after he returned from squandering his money on wine, women, and song, the older brother sulked and refused his father's pleas to join the party, saying,

> Look! All these years I've been slaving for you and never disobeyed your orders. Yet you never gave me even a young goat so I could celebrate with my friends. But when this son of yours who has squandered your property with prostitutes comes home, you kill the fattened calf for him! (Luke 15:29–30)

Jesus reveals the folly of the older brother's perspective through the words of his father: "My son … you are always with me, and everything I have is yours" (Luke 15:31). There's no indication, however, that the older brother ever joined the party.

We get the older brother's perspective naturally, as it is how the world system operates. From our earliest days picking teams on the playground, to hoping to be asked to the prom, to vying for the promotion or the membership in the club or sorority, we are constantly comparing ourselves, and being compared, to others. Such comparison and competition is not even intrinsically bad as it is the fuel of workable, albeit flawed, economic, social, and political systems. And any business owner or team coach wants his or her personnel or product to be better than the competitor's. Competition can be quite constructive. However, our constantly reinforced life experiences often result in a "lifeboat mentality" in which we believe we must make ourselves look better than the next person in order to earn or keep our place "on the boat" (Miller 2004, 113).

Jesus' message is that we have been set free from that pressure to make ourselves look better than other people in order to win God's approval and acceptance. He tells us that we are already accepted and loved by God, warts and all. We do *not* deserve it, and could never do enough to earn it, but God loves us anyway. That is what *grace* means. Not only that, but also Jesus says we must love others the same way, realizing we are all in the same boat, needing God's grace, which is sufficient to reach and save us all.

Christ's followers and his church must not operate the same as the world system. We cannot and still be distinct from the world as "salt" and "light." While we will inevitably find ourselves in the competitive marketplace or other institutions driven by constant comparisons between ourselves and other people, we are nevertheless freed to love them unconditionally, secure in our acceptance by God, and pointing them to that same realization of God's love and grace.

Principle 5: Don't make a show of your religion or bring attention to your own good deeds.

CHAPTER 7

Valuing the Spiritual

You could drown yourself in jewels like a thousand other fools
While you stand there looking down at what you've won
—Bruce Cockburn

While discussing our tendency to be consumed with what we eat or drink, or what we wear, Jesus asked his listeners, "Is not life more than food, and the body more than clothes" (Matthew 6:25)? Observing that God knows we need such basic necessities, Jesus urged his followers,

> But seek first his kingdom and his righteousness, and all
> these things will be given to you as well. (Matthew 6:33)

By telling his followers that there is something more important and beneficial to be pursued than material needs, namely God's kingdom and living rightly according to God's standards instead of our own, Jesus was teaching us a system of priorities that is completely different than that advanced by our culture.

The kingdom of God was an idea with which Jesus' Jewish audience would have been quite familiar. From the opening pages of the Torah through the historical books, psalms, and writings of the prophets, the promise of God to send a king who would establish an everlasting kingdom is the central theme of the scriptures they revered. These recorded God's promise to send someone "born of a woman" to deliver his people from the wreckage of sin and evil (Genesis 3:15), who would be from the descendants of Abraham (Genesis 12:1–3), specifically a ruler from the Tribe of Judah

(Genesis 49:10) and the lineage of King David (1 Chronicles 17:11–14). He would be born in Bethlehem (Micah 5:2) to a virgin, and be the very presence of God on earth (Isaiah 7:14), who would reign over his kingdom in justice and righteousness forever (Isaiah 9:6–7). The people, especially in their current context of the Roman oppression, eagerly awaited this Messiah and knew all about the kingdom.

Or so they thought. Throughout the three years of his public ministry, Jesus systematically turned their understanding of the kingdom of God upside down. For starters, he taught that "God is spirit, and his worshipers must worship in the Spirit and in truth" (John 4:24). It follows, then, that in order to "see or enter" God's kingdom, as Jesus said, our birth as humans is not sufficient—we must also experience a *spiritual* birth (John 3:3). Not only that, but also the kingdom foretold in their scriptures was unlike anything that anyone expected:

> Once, on being asked by the Pharisees when the kingdom of God would come, Jesus replied, "The coming of the kingdom of God is not something that can be observed, nor will people say, 'Here it is,' or 'There it is,' because the kingdom of God is in your midst." (Luke 17:20–21)

This kingdom of the true God-Spirit, comprised of worshipers who are spiritually alive and submitted to God's authority, is not visible to the naked eye but nonetheless present in our midst because it is a *spiritual* kingdom, transcending time and space. If we are to "seek it *first*," as Jesus instructs, it means that this spiritual reality and our participation in it is of more value than anything material, *even* the basic necessities of life.

But the value of the spiritual is not merely greater than the material things that consume our time, energy, and other resources, it is also more important than our *physical* bodies. In some of Jesus' harshest sounding words,

> If your right eye causes you to stumble, gouge it out and throw it away. It is better for you to lose one part of your body than for your whole body to be thrown into hell. And if your right hand causes you to stumble, cut it off

43

and throw it away. It is better for you to lose one part
of your body than for your whole body to go into hell.
(Matthew 5:29–30)

It could be observed that if we were to apply this strange teaching
literally, we might all be blind and without hands! So, is Jesus calling his
followers to self-mutilation? The fact of the matter is he does not let us off
that easy, warning that the cost of discipleship goes beyond our body parts
to our very lives:

> Then he said to them all: "Whoever wants to be my
> disciple must deny themselves and take up their cross
> daily and follow me. For whoever wants to save their life
> will lose it, but whoever loses their life for me will save it."
> (Luke 9:23–24)

As Dietrich Bonhoeffer observed, "When Christ calls a man, he bids him
come and die" (Bonhoeffer 1959, 89). What then, does Christ mean with
his words regarding our hands and eyes? As good teachers often do, he is
using hyperbole to make his point, which is that the spiritual realities of
life are more important than even our own bodies, just as they are more
important than the material things of life.

Throughout the history of the church, misguided people have used
Jesus' teaching to convey that our physical bodies and material things are
evil and should be regarded with disdain. Some of the letters in the New
Testament specifically address the error of that viewpoint. Frankly, one
need not engage in rigorous philosophical analysis to understand that it
is self-defeating to claim faith in God as the intrinsically good and all-
powerful Creator of all things, including our bodies and the world into
which we were born, while claiming that the bodies God gave us and the
material world all around us are inherently evil. If God is sovereign, as the
scriptures teach, then it is no mistake that we have the bodies we do, that
function and reproduce the way they do. We should celebrate this, within
contexts which please God, recognizing with gratitude as the psalmist did
that we are "fearfully and wonderfully made" (Psalm 139:14).

Likewise, it is no mistake that God has put each of us here and now, with the resources we have at our disposal. We are to be stewards of all our good gifts, recognizing that we are accountable for using them wisely. And as you and I embrace and celebrate the physical and material blessings of our lives, we must understand that they are less important and beneficial than the spiritual realities of God's kingdom and righteousness, which we are to value and seek above all.

Elsewhere, Jesus summed it all up in the rhetorical question, "What good is it for someone to gain the whole world, yet forfeit their soul?" (Mark 8:36). As the person I am, the way that God made me, I must come to see that my spiritual relationship with God, wherein I recognize God *as God* (Romans 1:21) and embrace His authority over me, is to be my highest priority in life. Of all the important things, this is the most important.

There are some *corollaries* that flow from this priority that have particular application to us in this culture. One is that we should not be consumed with our outward appearance. That is a difficult thing in a culture that bombards us, and especially young women, with hypersexualized, unrealistic, airbrushed, photoshopped standards of beauty. It is one thing to take care of ourselves and try to look good, but consider how much time, energy, and money we are encouraged to spend on fashion, diet, exercise, and even cosmetic surgery. The loud voices all around us proclaim that how we look and feel are the most important things and should be the focus of our lives, but Jesus said that is not so.

Another corollary to Jesus' priority system is that we must not live as if self-preservation is our highest value—it is not. He said, and showed, that some things are worth dying for:

> Greater love has no one than this: to lay down one's life for one's friends. (John 15:13).

> For whoever wants to save their life will lose it, but whoever loses their life for me and for the gospel will save it. (Mark 8:35).

While there is certainly an importance to self-protection and personal safety, sometimes, especially as parents, we communicate a message that preserving one's safety and well-being is all that matters. In one form, it may be the so-called "helicopter parent" who is always hovering around, insisting that he or she can and must insulate his or her kids from any possible physical or emotional hurt. It may be the parent who refuses to support a grown child's passionate decision to join the Peace Corps or the military or serve as a missionary in a distant, war-torn land. May we instead model and appropriately communicate to our children that there are some things worth sacrificing, fighting and even dying for, and teach them to discern what those are.

Beyond parenting, there are many voices that would have us live our lives in fear, urging us to cast our votes one way or another, spend our money on one form of protection after another, or seize a fleeting opportunity (whether illicit or not) because we might never get it again. Ultimately, these pander to our fear of dying, and the message of Jesus is that we need no longer fear death—he has set us free from that universal fear (John 11:25, 10:28–29; Hebrews 2:14–15). God's perfect love casts out all our fear (1 John 4:18).

Another corollary to the priority of the spiritual over the material or physical is that what we allow inside our hearts and minds can cause us more harm than we realize. Jesus said,

> Listen to me, everyone, and understand this. Nothing outside a person can defile them by going into them. Rather, it is what comes out of a person that defiles them… For it is from within, out of a person's heart, that evil thoughts come—sexual immorality, theft, murder, adultery, greed, malice, deceit, lewdness, envy, slander, arrogance and folly. All these evils come from inside and defile a person. (Mark 7:14–23)

This is why *ideas* are so important—they are seeds that could well take root and grow into full-blown actions, and that is true for individuals as well as collective groups such as societies or nations. Examples of the latter are seen in structural racism, hate groups, and genocide, all of which are prevalent in the world today. And while there is an equality of people before God, all of whom are to be loved and treated with dignity and respect, the same is not true of ideas. Some ideas are inferior to others and should be recognized as such, and even demolished (2 Corinthians 10:5), for if we are cavalier about them, we could find ourselves, individually or collectively, further along a path of behavior than we ever thought we would go. That is why Jesus warns us against illicit actions at their root, teaching, for example, that it is anger that can grow into murder, and lustful thoughts that can lead to adultery (Matthew 5:21–27).

By embracing the priority system that Jesus taught, wherein we regard our spiritual health as more important than even the material or physical dimensions of our lives, we will safeguard our hearts and minds from lesser thoughts or behaviors that would inevitably lead to lesser experiences than those of a full and abundant life. And, we will find the resulting peace, joy, and love to which Jesus invites us all through the pursuit of life his way.

> ***Principle 6: Value the spiritual realities of life even more than material or physical realities.***

CHAPTER 8

Avoiding Worry

So why worry now?
—Dire Straits

I live in a city on the Florida coast in which visits to our beautiful beaches are a regular part of life. From time to time, I meet people who still will not step into the ocean because they saw the movie *Jaws* and remain terrified of sharks. It seems that the fear of being eaten alive is deep and long-lasting, and the *tiny* odds of an encounter with a shark are enough to keep them stuck on the beach, no matter how refreshing or fun it might be to splash around in the waves.

In the same passage in which Jesus taught his followers the higher value and priority they should place on spiritual realities over those which are material or physical, he addressed the major obstacle to living that way: *worry.* If we are honest, many of us allow worry to consume or "eat us up," which, among other things, keeps us from many joyful, exhilarating experiences in life. Jesus says we must not live that way.

> Therefore I tell you, do not worry about your life, what you will eat or drink; or about your body, what you will wear. Is not life more than food, and the body more than clothes? … Can any one of you by worrying add a single hour to your life? … So do not worry, saying, 'What shall we eat?' or 'What shall we drink?' or 'What shall we wear?' For the pagans run after all these things, and your heavenly Father knows that you need them. But seek first

his kingdom and his righteousness, and all these things
will be given to you as well. Therefore do not worry about
tomorrow, for tomorrow will worry about itself. Each day
has enough trouble of its own. (Matthew 6:25–34)

Jesus' reference to trouble in his summarizing statement reminds us that worry at its essence is anticipating negative events or circumstances that may or may not happen. It is engaging in what-if thinking, and because it is anticipatory, it hinders us from being present in *this* moment. Worry, says Jesus, accomplishes nothing and keeps our focus off of the challenges at hand. It exacts a spiritual toll, too, as it is contrary to *faith*, which is fundamental to embracing the spiritual realities of life. And, as we know from our own experiences, it is also detrimental to our emotional and even physical well-being. Who among us has not felt, or seen another, sick with worry?

No wonder Jesus' exhortation to his listeners, "Do not worry," is emphatic and repeated. And the examples he gives reveal that it is also broad and categorical. We are clearly told to not worry about material things, even the basic necessities such as food, drink, and clothing. Likewise, he makes clear that we are not to worry about tomorrow, that is, the future. By pointing out that none of us by worry can add a single hour to our lives, however, Jesus is also telling us to not worry about things we cannot control. Many things that would tempt us to worry fall into that category. Will the economy recover? Will I develop Alzheimer's disease? Do my classmates think I am weird? Will an unstable regime get its hands on nuclear weapons? If I am not to worry about material things, or the future, or that which I cannot control, what is left for me to worry about? Obviously nothing, and that is Jesus' point.

His command may be clear and all-inclusive, but *how* do we not worry? When my wife, Sally, and I were unexpectedly pregnant with our fourth child, a standard prenatal test in our first trimester came back in the range for a genetic abnormality. Upon further testing, it was confirmed that the baby boy we were carrying had trisomy 21, Down syndrome. Even though Sally has a degree and specialized training and experience working with such special-needs children, and one of her older sisters has Down syndrome, the definitive diagnosis rocked our world and called into question all of our views about terminating pregnancy. We were stunned and unsure of our next step. The thoughts that consumed our minds and anguished conversations were about what was to come. Even our attempts at prayer during this personal crisis seemed to lead us back to the same questions. How will we care for this boy? Will he be high functioning? Will he have other physical problems often attendant with Down syndrome? Will he go to school? Be able to read and write? Will he always live with us? Who will take care of him when we are gone, etc.?

A close friend met with us quickly upon our receiving the news and listened patiently as we poured out our concerns. He then gently observed that we were projecting and compressing all of the potential problems of our son's lifetime into *this moment now* and trying to make our decision from that perspective. He reminded us that life—anyone's life, whether with special needs or not—cannot be lived that way. The focus must be on living *this day*, not some days ahead that may or may not come. That was also Jesus' point when he said, "Each day has enough trouble of its own." Embracing this perspective is essential, and I could see the application immediately to other momentous decisions in my life.

Sally and I had been married for nearly ten years at the time (and over thirty now), and although we have had our struggles and crises, we are blessed and happy together. There is no question in my mind that she has patiently made me a better man. I cannot imagine, however, if some well-intentioned person had pulled me aside before I stepped to the altar on our wedding day and told me, in the spirit of "full disclosure," all that was in store for us as a couple on the road ahead. I would have been so terrified I would have run the other way! But if I had done so, I would have missed out on one of the greatest blessings in my life. Likewise, if Sally and I had elected to terminate our pregnancy, we would have never experienced the sheer delight that Collin brings to our lives and the lives of many around us. He has truly made our lives richer than we could have ever imagined.

Jesus' lesson is clear—we simply cannot condense the trouble of a lifetime into this moment. It accomplishes nothing, and the emotional, spiritual and physical impact it makes on us is highly detrimental. Moreover, as I have seen in the examples of my sweet wife and our son, Collin, my quality and experience of life would have been greatly diminished if I had given in to such worry.

Remember also that in this passage, Jesus is teaching us about priorities, that is, we are to value things spiritual, specifically God's kingdom and right-standing with Him, more than things material or physical. The key to not worrying is to embrace this priority system. Doing so, we realize (by faith) what Jesus explains—our Heavenly Father cares about us and He knows our material and physical needs.

This is a theme echoed by the apostle Paul in his letter to the Philippians: "And my God will meet all your needs according to the riches of his glory in Christ Jesus" (Philippians 4:19). The Greek word for "worry" used to recount Jesus' sermon is *merimnao*, which is also a word used by Paul in the same letter: "Do not be anxious about anything, but in every situation, by prayer and petition, with thanksgiving, present your requests to God (Philippians 4:6).

The essential truth is clear: since God cares about us and supplies our needs, we need not worry, but instead look to Him to provide. And because God accepts us and listens to us, we do so *with gratitude*. A mind-set of gratefully "accepting our acceptance," recognizing in faith that God cares for us and will meet our needs, becomes the foundation from which we can throw away our worries/anxieties, whether about material things, the future, or other things we cannot control. This antidote to worry was succinctly expressed by the apostle Peter when he wrote, "Cast all your anxiety on him because he cares for you" (1 Peter 5:7).

This perspective and approach to life that helps us avoid worry is obviously grounded in faith. That should be no surprise because there can be no interaction or relationship with God without faith (Hebrews 11:6). We tend to "spiritualize" faith, however, and overlook the fact that *every world view*, whether theistic, agnostic, or atheistic, starts with faith, because each requires the acceptance of foundational presuppositions that cannot be empirically proven and are not self-evident.

Jesus had a lot to say about faith, and some may be surprised to know that he taught the amount or size of our faith is not what is important (Luke 17:5–6). He also cited a pagan soldier as an example of great faith (Matthew 8:5–10) and honored the faith of a man who simultaneously expressed real doubts (Mark 9:23–25). And his closest followers, like Peter, for example, exhibited a faith that was wavering and unsteady (Matthew 14:28–31). But that is often the nature of faith. I may be terrified to fly, filled with uncertainty as to whether the massive machine put together, inspected and operated by various people, all of whom I know nothing about, will get me safely to my destination. By boarding the airplane, however, even reluctantly, I am exercising my faith that it will. What is the essential quality of faith, then? It is acting as if what I claim to believe is true. And as Jesus pointedly reminded his followers, our actions reveal the genuineness of our faith more than our words ever will.

With respect to the things we tend to worry about—material needs, the future, and things we cannot control—we must live as if there really is a God who exists and cares about us. We must take the next step today as if God really does hold our future in loving and capable hands and will supply our needs, as promised. We go about our lives as if God really is present with us and will never leave us, and that whatever happens—even if we die—it is not the end and God will be with us still. If we live as if these promises are true, even while possibly experiencing moments of doubt or uncertainty, taking one wavering step at a time, we will be walking by faith and overcoming worry. It is the next step—not those down the road—that leads to a life free from worry.

Beyond the essence of what it means to live by faith, however, is the undeniable quality that such living brings to a person's experience of life. This point was driven home to me while travelling in the Philippines as an intern in the Wheaton College Human Needs and Global Resources (HNGR) program. On one particular three-day trip in the southern island of Mindanao, I set out alone on a public jitney, realizing that I would have to stay overnight along the way but not knowing where or with whom. There is something exhilarating about "going while not knowing" and counting on and experiencing the kindness and generosity of strangers who took me in.

On another occasion, I had to travel many miles over a rural mountain road that was notoriously treacherous and narrow, and found out my only transportation option was the infamous "Philippine Rabbit"—the most dilapidated bus I had ever seen—in which the dirt road was literally visible through the floorboards. When the crowded bus arrived at the roadside queue, the door swung open, and I saw the driver in his head bandana and mirror shades grin at me, I had to consciously subdue much internal resistance while boarding the bus with great "fear and trembling."

The ride over those narrow mountain roads at breakneck speed was even more harrowing than I had imagined, but I cannot recall many instances in my life in which I felt more *alive*. In a somewhat quirky way, these events in my past remind me that living by faith really enhances my experience of life, which I am convinced is a part of the life to the full that Jesus said he came to bring (John 10:10).

The life of a Christ-follower involves exchanging the futile, destructive energy of worry for the hopeful step into the unknown that is faith. Jesus invites us to trust him and take that step—to let go of and leave to God that which we can do nothing about. The result in the immediate term will be replacing futility and frustration with hope and exhilaration. And if Jesus can be trusted, we will also experience peace, secure in his promise that he has ultimately overcome the troubles of this world (John 16:33), as well as life with him that extends beyond our time here.

> *Principle 7: Instead of worrying about the future, material things, or that which you cannot control, trust that God loves you and will provide.*

CHAPTER 9

Keeping Your Word

You made me promises, promises
You knew you'd never keep
—Naked Eyes

Nobody likes a liar, and few would ever admit to being one. Nevertheless, all of us are exposed every day to calamity and dysfunction caused by lies in the marketplace, halls of power, and our offices, neighborhoods and homes. In election season, our local newspaper runs a column called "Fact Check" in which the TV ads of all candidates in a particular race are vetted for accuracy. No one scores well.

Of course, like political candidates seem to do universally, we all rationalize when we take liberty with the truth. Typically, we relabel it, perhaps describing what we are doing as only "stretching the truth" or merely withholding information that is unimportant. If we feel cornered, we might own up to a "fib" or say we were "just fudging," or even resort to the age-old description of telling a "little white lie." In some circles, we might get fancy and refer to an "alternative narrative" or talk of aiming for "plausible deniability."

I have a friend whose mother had a deteriorating condition that left her exceedingly difficult to live with for many, many years. Nevertheless, his father stayed married to her in spite of the challenging and unpleasant circumstances. His father was not particularly religious, and toward the end my friend, a pastor, asked him, "Why have you stayed with her for so long Dad?" His answer: "Because I said I would." My friend told me he felt like taking off his shoes because he knew that he was standing on holy ground. Indeed, he was.

Jesus made clear that people who seek to live the way he taught will be people who keep their word. He zeroed in on the common tactic of religious people to make vows and reference God or things spiritual to add validity to their words:

> But I tell you, do not swear an oath at all: either by heaven, for it is God's throne; or by the earth, for it is his footstool; or by Jerusalem, for it is the city of the Great King. And do not swear by your head, for you cannot make even one hair white or black. All you need to say is simply 'Yes' or 'No'; anything beyond this comes from the evil one. (Matthew 5:34–37)

No matter how you analyze it, our intent when we play the God card is to add credibility to whatever we are saying. We are, in effect, saying that "we *really* mean it *this* time." The fact is, however, that invoking God to vouch for our veracity only serves to cheapen God. That is because if we were truly people of our word, we would not need the self-serving endorsement. And because we do not always do what we say, dragging God into our broken promises makes *Him* look bad. Jesus said not to do that.

We might think his admonitions are a little strange and do not apply in modern times. However, this technique of invoking God and heaven is as much a part of our culture as it was for Christ's listeners. For example, how many times have we heard or said with great aplomb, "I *swear* to God," or "As God is my witness"? And how is that different than "swearing by heaven"? It is clearly not. Even leaving God out of it and resorting to "swearing by one's head" might seem odd to our ears until we consider familiar modern attempts to enhance credibility such as "I cross my heart, hope to die," or "I swear on my mother's grave!" Just as we cannot truly change the color of one of our hairs from white to black, all such references are nonsensical or about things that we cannot possibly control. Jesus points out that these are just *meaningless words*, and if we are people of our word, we would have no need to add them.

Instead of such self-serving and meaningless endorsements, Jesus teaches us to say what we mean and mean what we say. If we mean yes, say it, and if we mean no, say that. The fact is, a commitment to this simple change by any person will be noticed by others in his or her life. For some of us, it may take time to overcome past lies, and there may be some we never fully live down. However, it will quickly become known by the people with whom you have ongoing contact that your word can be trusted if you simply make it your practice to say what you mean and mean what you say.

Note that this principle goes beyond merely telling the truth. Jesus certainly emphasized truth, claiming that he was, in fact, "the truth" (John 14:6). In one encounter, he pointedly gave some very religious people of his day a piece of his mind, emphasizing who their no-good, lying "Daddy" was:

> You belong to your father, the devil, and you want to carry out your father's desires. He was a murderer from the beginning, not holding to the truth, for there is no truth in him. When he lies, he speaks his native language, for he is a liar and the father of lies. (John 8:44)

Additionally, Jesus often started his teaching on a particular topic by saying, "I tell you the truth." He also promised to send his followers a helper after he left, the "Spirit of truth," who would lead them into all truth (John 16:13). Clearly, Jesus was very much concerned with the truth.

By telling his followers to let their "yes be yes" and their "no be no," however, Jesus goes beyond their telling the truth to being people who mean what they say and can be counted on to *keep their word*. In the context of making oaths, the words are invariably about actions, that is, something they would or would not *do*. If we *do what we say*, then our word becomes our bond. And if we say something, people should be able to count on us meaning what we say and not something else (as if we have our fingers crossed or would be playing some word trick). When we approach our words and promises in such a way, we do not need gimmicky bluster and emphasis. Conversely, if what we say is at odds with what we mean, this is *duplicity*. And if our words are at odds with what we do, this is *hypocrisy*. Either way, we will soon be rightly regarded by others as untrustworthy. But when we mean what we say and then do it, *even when* it is no longer advantageous or costs more than expected, it goes beyond honesty (telling the truth) to the quality of *integrity*. What we say is not different than what we mean or do—it is consistent through and through.

Imagine if all or even most of us who claim to be Christians were people of our word, keeping our marriage vows, performing our ends of business deals, and fulfilling our financial commitments. The incidents within the church of infidelity and divorce, financial fraud, sexual abuse and cover-up, business swindles, and the like would virtually disappear. This single change alone would do more to reflect positively on Jesus Christ and cause others to be interested in him and his message than dozens of sermons ever could.

Principle 8: Be a person of your word.

CHAPTER 10

Serving Others

Know your rights, these are your rights
—The Clash

In Western culture, and especially in America, we are acutely aware of individual rights. In fact, the protection of individual rights that were regarded by the Founding Fathers of America as fundamentally God-endowed in all people, and so obvious as to be self-evident, was the prime catalyst for the system of constitutional government they crafted that many of us enjoy today. We are taught from our earliest days in school to recognize the sacrifice of many before us who fought and perhaps died protecting those rights, and the unrelenting drum beat of individual rights continues three centuries later, even as we engage in lively debate regarding the breadth and scope of those rights. We cherish our individual rights, and for good reason.

For citizens of a kingdom that transcends any national boundary, however, comprised of people from every tribe, nation, and tongue, the perspective on individual rights is very different. Jesus made that clear when, in the context of a society subject to an oppressive foreign (Roman) occupation, he taught his followers to *not* insist on their rights, but rather to practice deference toward others.

> But I tell you, do not resist an evil person. If anyone slaps
> you on the right cheek, turn to them the other cheek also.
> And if anyone wants to sue you and take your shirt, hand

over your coat as well. If anyone forces you to go one mile,
go with them two miles. (Matthew 5:39–41)

From this familiar passage, we acknowledge even today the virtue of "turning the other cheek". Although we usually gloss over Jesus' illustration involving litigation, we do speak of a person "going the extra mile" and usually mean it as a compliment in recognition of him or her doing more than what is expected or required in a particular circumstance.

Jesus' extra-mile illustration was specifically in the context of one person *serving* another. While the first mile is "forced" service, the second is voluntary and unexpected, and Jesus repeatedly called his followers to such service of others. He told them clearly, "Anyone who wants to be first must be the very last, and the servant of all" (Mark 9:35), and he stunned them the night before his death by washing their feet, saying that they should follow his example and do the same for each other (John 13:14–15). Jesus' whole life was about service to others.

The early church recognized the deferential mindset essential to applying this principle of service:

Do nothing out of selfish ambition or vain conceit. Rather,
in humility value others above yourselves, not looking to
your own interests but each of you to the interests of the
others. (Philippians 2:3–4)

In order to serve others, we cannot demand our own rights because the very act of service involves subordinating our interests to those of others.

If we consider again Jesus' call to willingly forgo our own rights in the context of his specific illustrations, we learn more. A common objection to Jesus' illustration of turning the other cheek is "I'm not going to be anyone's doormat," or "God doesn't call me to be a weakling and not fight back and defend myself." We cannot escape the fact, however, that one of the very examples given by Jesus of a person not demanding his rights is when he is physically struck in the face by another. Moreover, that is exactly the approach Jesus took when he was struck and mocked while appearing before the religious and political rulers on the day of his death (Matthew 26:67, 27:27–31). And while the image of Jesus being battered leaves us with many impressions, being a weakling is not one of them, and his example of not resisting violence with more violence has been followed by many great people and literally changed the world.

Is this then a call to pacifism? Although some Christ-followers ultimately reach that conclusion, I do not think it is. We have an example in the Bible of Jesus getting physical in clearing the Temple (Mark 11:15–17), and that shows me there are some things worth fighting for. Moreover, it is difficult to imagine that the ultimate example of love given by Jesus, sacrificing one's life for another (John 15:13), would never occur in the context of physical conflict and violence.

Another context that Jesus specifically illustrated was litigation, both in the reference above where he said to "give your coat also" to the one who is suing you for "your shirt," as well as the following verses from the same sermon:

> Settle matters quickly with your adversary who is taking you to court. Do it while you are still together on the way, or your adversary may hand you over to the judge, and the judge may hand you over to the officer, and you may be thrown into prison. Truly I tell you, you will not get out until you have paid the last penny. (Matthew 5:25–26)

While the practical wisdom of Jesus' illustration may be somewhat lost on us today since we are long removed (at least in America) from the days of a literal "debtor's prison," the principle of not demanding one's own rights in deference to others is still an underlying mindset that the early church grasped that remains quite applicable:

> Is it possible that there is nobody among you wise enough to judge a dispute between believers? But instead, one brother takes another to court—and this in front of unbelievers! The very fact that you have lawsuits among you means you have been completely defeated already. Why not rather be wronged? Why not rather be cheated? Instead, you yourselves cheat and do wrong, and you do this to your brothers and sisters. (1 Corinthians 6:5–8)

Given what I do for a living as a trial lawyer, I have had numerous opportunities to discuss such passages with people who claim to be Christians who are contemplating suing others who identify themselves the same way. Invariably, the person who decides to proceed with a lawsuit rationalizes his or her decision by concluding in essence that, notwithstanding the prohibition in scripture of one Christian suing another, there is "*no way* that the other person is *really* a Christian given how he treated me."

This thought process misses completely what the early church understood: that lawsuits between Christians give people who are watching a reason to conclude that there is no real love or unity among Jesus' followers, which is *exactly the opposite* of what he wanted for us. Jesus said that it is by our *love* for each other that people will know we are his disciples (John 13:35), and it is our *unity*—how we get along—that God will use to demonstrate to a watching world that Jesus was sent by God:

> My prayer is not for them alone. I pray also for those who will believe in me through their message, that all of them may be one, Father, just as you are in me and I am in you. May they also be in us so that the world may believe that you have sent me. I have given them the glory that you gave me, that they may be one as we are one— I in them and you in me—so that they may be brought to complete unity. Then the world will know that you sent me and have loved them even as you have loved me. (John 17:20–23)

Indeed, it is better for us to suffer a wrong than risk detracting from that message. Of course, the rationalization to sue anyway since the other person could not possibly be a believer also overlooks that Jesus taught us to defer even when sued by an "evil" person, so the parsing of these passages will not overcome the obvious.

So is there a place for litigation by Christ-followers? While all of us need to decide for ourselves in each specific context, I believe there is. I have seen people bravely enter that unpleasant, time-consuming, and expensive process to stand up for the rights and protection of others. For example, I know men and women who have sued employers who terminated or mistreated them for discriminatory reasons in order to prevent them from doing that to anyone else. I am aware of inventors or artists who have had their creative and intellectual property stolen by individuals or companies who will continue their unscrupulous ways unless stopped. I have seen parents severely injured in car accidents recover damages from an at-fault driver's insurance company (that received a premium and issued coverage for that very possibility) so that they and their kids were provided for. I know many people who courageously decided to exercise their individual rights by suing companies that would otherwise go unfettered in their greed and disregard for consumer safety.

Is our system in America perfect? Of course not—it is populated by imperfect people. Is it possibly vulnerable to fraudulent scams and other abuse? Certainly, but I know of nothing better that will get the attention of individuals and companies who would otherwise make a habit of preying on others without having a second thought. Exercising one's individual rights out of concern for others strikes me as consistent with Jesus' teachings and example.

A related, but different, legal context that may cause us to question Jesus' principle of turning the other cheek is when I am a victim of crime. However, in the criminal law system, most serious crimes involve no choice by the victim whether to prosecute as the crime is also considered an offense to the state. As noted earlier, the state is not called to follow Jesus' way; individuals are. The scriptures teach that the state is ordained by God "to punish those who do wrong and to commend those who do right" (1 Peter 2:14).

But serious crimes *do* often involve sentencing input by the victim or her family, and less serious crimes (note that Jesus' example of striking you on the cheek would be classified as a "misdemeanor battery" today) often involve a decision by the victim as to whether to press charges. In such instances where my input may be determinative, remembering that we as individuals are called by Jesus to forgive others (even our enemies), similar considerations regarding how my decision may impact other people would seem to apply, as well. For example, would prosecution or a long sentence recommendation protect others from being victimized? Will the perpetrator be more likely to "reform" in jail or prison or not? Prayerful consideration of such questions will nudge our focus onto God and others and help guard against us giving in to a desire for revenge or seeking our pound of flesh.

What about we who are Christ-followers demanding our rights as citizens, if we are so fortunate to live in a country that affords them? At the outset, we should notice that the idea of *demanding* usually reveals something about the attitude of our hearts that seems contrary to anything that Jesus taught or showed. In fact, he modeled not doing so before Herod and Pilate.

Are we to see that as a blanket prohibition? The apostle Paul certainly did not when he demanded a hearing before Caesar, which was his right as a Roman citizen (Acts 23–26). But did Paul do so in order to save his own skin? No, in a stroke of brilliance he exercised his right as the means to fulfill his calling to be God's witness in Rome:

> The following night the Lord stood near Paul and said, "Take courage! As you have testified about me in Jerusalem, so you must also testify in Rome." (Acts 23:11)

In other words, his actions were not for himself but in service of others. This is the key context for insisting on rights that I may have as a citizen. So, too, in exercising my rights as a litigant; it is appropriate for me to ask—am I protecting others by doing so (my family, a specific group of people, other consumers, etc.)?

Another context in which Jesus taught specifically about deferring our individual rights is when we are in positions of authority over others. Examples of this might be if I am the boss at work, a customer in a restaurant, or airline passenger at a ticket counter. Jesus says that his followers are not to use their positions like weapons or "lord it over" others; rather, we are to serve others:

> Jesus called them together and said, "You know that those who are regarded as rulers of the Gentiles lord it over them, and their high officials exercise authority over them. Not so with you. Instead, whoever wants to become great among you must be your servant, and whoever wants to be first must be slave of all. For even the Son of Man did not come to be served, but to serve, and to give his life as a ransom for many. (Mark 10:42–45)

I believe it is a very important diagnostic exercise for each of us to ask ourselves: how do I treat service people such as waitresses, secretaries, help-desk clerks? Do I treat them with dignity, consideration, and respect? Or do I make sure to let them know who is in charge? Do I say, or even *think*, "Do you know who I am?" We can tell a lot about ourselves and others when we consider how we exercise the upper hand. One who seeks to live like Jesus will, even in the context of positions of power, show kindness and concern for people who are in subservient positions. We will not be disrespectful, even if we are duty bound to insist that they properly perform their jobs. This is not a mysterious concept—we all know very well what it looks like when a boss or a customer is unreasonably demanding, condescending, or on a power trip. Jesus calls us to a higher bar.

Principle 9: Instead of demanding your own rights, serve others.

CHAPTER 11

Addressing Conflict

We can work it out
—The Beatles

Few of us like interpersonal conflict, and some of us avoid it at all costs. The problem is that life is fundamentally about relationships, whether we like it or not. To illustrate that basic fact, consider that each of us is born to parents we did not choose. Even if we wished mightily, for some reason, that they were not our parents, it does not change the fact that they are. If we (hypothetically) tried to disown them, or cut off all communication and interaction, it still does not mean that we are no longer related. It means at most that our relationship is *broken*.

Even beyond our parents (or siblings or children), most of us have little, if any, say about who our neighbors or coworkers will be. If we *could* control that somehow, we still cannot avoid relating with people we encounter in our kids' school, the grocery store, our athletic teams, social clubs, trade groups, or other organizations. We simply cannot escape relationships, and relationships are messy and constantly ripe for conflict. That is because we are all imperfect people with a bent toward self-interest. And while it may be our preference and certainly seem easier, Christ-followers must not ignore, avoid, or cover-up the conflicts that inevitably arise in our personal relationships.

In discussing common scenarios of such interpersonal conflict, Jesus shows that we must not use the difficulty or unpleasantness of becoming involved as a reason to be passive or disengage. Rather, we are called to lovingly confront and address interpersonal conflict. The first scenario is when you have wronged someone or know they have something against you. Note that this is the flip side of a situation where someone has wronged you or you have something against them. Jesus' prescription in such circumstances is, as we have already discussed, that we *must forgive*. When *we are the wrong-doer*, however, our consideration of whether to forgive makes no sense as we are not in a position to forgive. Instead, Jesus taught us the following:

> Therefore, if you are offering your gift at the altar and there remember that your brother or sister has something against you, leave your gift there in front of the altar. First go and be reconciled to them; then come and offer your gift. Settle matters quickly with your adversary who is taking you to court. Do it while you are still together on the way... (Matthew 5:23–25)

There are several features to the process of addressing interpersonal conflict here. First, we are to take the initiative and make the first move. I must not wait for the other person to come to me, but instead I must *go* to him or her, which also implies doing so *personally* and *privately*. This requires a humble recognition that I have done wrong, or at least that I know the other person believes I have (there certainly could be circumstances when it is a misperception on their part). When we find ourselves refusing to make the first move, it is almost always grounded in pride. How often do relationships remain broken because no one is willing to reach out to the other? Jesus says we must make that first move.

Another feature is that we must do so *quickly*. That is, we are to keep short accounts with other people. Christ-followers must not delay and try to sweep things under the rug, hoping the matter will go away. By personally addressing the matter quickly, we do our part to see that the conflict does not simmer, fester or grow larger and possibly out of proportion. The wisdom of addressing interpersonal conflict quickly is illustrated by the apostle Paul in his letter to the church at Ephesus:

In your anger do not sin. Do not let the sun go down
while you are still angry, and do not give the devil a
foothold. (Ephesians 4:26–27)

I was advised early in my marriage that I should never go to bed angry.
That is certainly good advice for me as a husband, but as I have learned,
it is wisdom that has also served me well in parenting my children, in
my relationships with friends and neighbors, and in my working and
professional life. Christ-followers must be committed to move quickly to
address obstacles and brokenness in our relationships.

Another important feature in Jesus' illustration of the man dropping
everything at the altar is the recognition that conflict in our relationships
with others impacts our relationships with God. That is why seeking
reconciliation is so important, even more important than the acts of
worship in which the man was engaged! Wouldn't our relationships be
healthier and stronger if we made it a top priority to seek and pursue
reconciliation whenever we have wronged another? Jesus is telling his
followers that this priority must start with them, reminding us again that
he is more interested in love and unity being displayed in the church that
bears his name than in any religious act or sacrifice of service to him. The
apostle John said it this way:

Whoever claims to love God yet hates a brother or sister is
a liar. For whoever does not love their brother and sister,
whom they have seen, cannot love God, whom they have
not seen. And he has given us this command: Anyone
who loves God must also love their brother and sister. (1
John 4:20–21)

But what about when we have wronged people who do not claim to be
Christ-followers? The same principle of us quickly making the first move
toward reconciliation applies, even if for different reasons, as Jesus shows
in the interaction with the man and his adversary on their way to court.

Sometimes a situation may be too raw, and the other person is not yet
receptive to my attempt to reconcile. While that is something I cannot
control, I must not use it as an excuse for failing to do what I can. As the

apostle Paul reminded the church at Rome, "If it is possible, as far as it depends on you, live at peace with everyone" (Romans 12:18). The part that depends on us is quickly going to the person to try and make amends. We must do our part, as well as we can, to be reconciled with those who have something against us. If they refuse, they will at least know that we valued the relationship enough to seek reconciliation. And if we are rebuffed in our attempt, we should look for other opportunities to *try again* as it may be that they just need some more time.

A second scenario in Jesus' teaching about addressing interpersonal conflict is when we see a fellow Christ-follower committing sin.

> If your brother or sister sins, go and point out their fault, just between the two of you. If they listen to you, you have won them over. But if they will not listen, take one or two others along, so that "every matter may be established by the testimony of two or three witnesses." If they still refuse to listen, tell it to the church; and if they refuse to listen even to the church, treat them as you would a pagan or a tax collector. (Matthew 18:15–17)

Note that some manuscripts say "sins *against you*." This is probably correct, but there are certainly situations where we could see a brother or sister committing apparent wrong against another without the other's knowledge. In such situations, other scriptures make it clear that doing nothing is not an option (James 5:19–20; 1 Corinthians 5:1–12). For example, what if you saw a sister stealing from your friend? Or what if you and your wife are friends with a couple from church, and while travelling on business, you see the man sharing intimate moments with another woman? Should you really do or say nothing?

Although it is hardly pleasant to get involved, doing so should not offend our sensibilities, and Jesus makes clear that we must. And always remember the goal in our involvement: Jesus says it is to win him over. It is not to embarrass or shame the other person. Simply put, when we overcome our hesitancy and do what Jesus taught on this issue, we are trying to discretely bring a sister or brother back from a path that will lead to brokenness, pain, and heartache for them and others. Such actions, humbly taken, are in the best interest of the sinning brother or sister, and that is the very definition of love, which Jesus said is the mark of his followers (John 13:35).

As to the process for addressing such situations, note that it again starts by you making the first move and personally going to the person in private. This respects his or her dignity and spares them unnecessary embarrassment. It also gives him or her opportunity to explain their actions. Perhaps there is a misperception on our part that is easily clarified. In such an instance, even though there might be some initial embarrassment or offense, the brother or sister will likely come to appreciate that you cared enough to confront them (personally and privately). If there was no mistake, and the fellow believer admits and turns back from his or her wrong, then that is the end of your role in it. You have lovingly addressed the issue.

If, on the other hand, they admit the wrong but refuse to repent or turn back from it, you are to involve one or two others who will go with you and try again. If he or she still refuses to repent, you and the witnesses are to tell it to the church. As a practical matter, if you or the other witnesses are not church leaders, you should tell the appropriate leaders and let them decide how to communicate it further. If even telling the church does not work to make the brother or sister turn from his or her wrong, Jesus said you are to treat them as a "tax collector" or nonbeliever.

The last step in the process begs the question, how is the church called to treat nonbelievers? According to what Jesus taught and demonstrated, they should be treated by Christ-followers with love, grace, dignity, and respect. It also could not have been lost on Jesus' listeners that one of his inner circle of disciples, Matthew, was a tax collector (Matthew 10:3), and Jesus made it a point, much to the chagrin of his religious critics, to visit and even eat with tax collectors (Luke 19:1–9). Therefore, I believe that this last step in the process that Jesus outlined is not a prescription for shunning, as practiced in some churches.

On the other hand, it should be obvious that the manner in which a person who is a member of a church can participate and fellowship with his church family is different, more familiar and intimate, than someone who is not. Just like with any family, company or social group, the kind of things you do and share with each other are different than those you do with someone outside the group. It makes no sense for a church to continue to function as usual when, for example, a member or leader is in an open adulterous affair and his wife, also a member, sits in the congregation with a broken heart. This negatively impacts the whole church body and tarnishes Christ's name, which it bears. It is appropriate and wise to treat a person who professes to be a Christ-follower, yet refuses to turn from his or her sin even though they have been lovingly and discretely confronted on several occasions, as if they are no longer a part of the church.

It is not unlike a situation in which a brokenhearted father tells a son struggling with substance abuse, who has refused repeated efforts of intervention, that he cannot live at home and disrupt the rest of the family if he is unwilling to get treatment. The earnest hope is that the prodigal son comes to his senses, gets the help he needs, and returns to those who love him, even if it takes tough love to get his attention. So, too, with a member of a church family who refuses, in spite of repeated pleas, to turn from an open and obvious sinful path. The goal of the process that Jesus prescribes is that the person leave his or her destructive behavior and be restored to the church body.

We cannot be so literal regarding Jesus' teaching about addressing interpersonal conflict to conclude that it only applies to the two common scenarios discussed above. Rather, the examples he gives of people taking the initiative to quickly, personally, and privately address matters with others provide practical guidance for dealing with *any* interpersonal conflict. The point is clear: personal relationships are a fundamental part of life, and because we are all imperfect people, interpersonal conflict will inevitably arise. Christ-followers must not ignore, avoid, or cover up such conflict but instead must lovingly address it as Jesus prescribed. This is the hard work of reconciliation and restoration, and although the task may be unpleasant or difficult, our mandate to love compels us to do what we can.

Principle 10: Lovingly confront and address relational conflict.

CHAPTER 12

Avoiding Greed

But you're gonna have to serve somebody
—Bob Dylan

For a brief time, there was an establishment near my house called the "Die Rich Club." It apparently failed to achieve the proprietor's goal as it went out of business. I never went in to check it out, but I was always struck by the name. It reminded me of the bumper stickers you still see from time to time: "The one who dies with the most toys wins." In a world with unfathomable economic disparity, where 80 percent of the global population lives on less than ten US dollars per day, and more than 1.3 billion people wallow in extreme poverty (less than $1.25 USD per day), we should be more thoughtful than to proclaim membership in such a club or display a bumper sticker like that.

In America, where the economic system is premised on people ever-consuming and acquiring, we have recently seen that a slowdown in the production and consumption of goods can have dire and far-reaching consequences. This logical result has been understood by several keen observers of our society, including Dr. Tony Campolo *nearly two decades ago* while he contemplated buying "that perfect gift" for someone at Christmas time:

> There is something very important we Americans have to do. Buy! We have to buy the stuff that our system produces. And we have to keep on buying. The megatons of consumer goods that flow out of our factories annually must be purchased fast and furiously. If they are not, factories will

close, workers will become unemployed, and everything will stop. … If people like you and me, whose needs have already been met, are going to keep America going, we are going to have to buy what we don't need. And we are going to have to buy what we don't need in larger and larger quantities. As absurd as all of this may seem, the survival of our way of life depends on this. (Campolo 1994, 35–36)

It is no surprise, then, that billions of dollars are spent by producers in marketing and advertising in order to convince us consumers to buy that which we do not need.

Given these realities, it would be easy for materialism to creep into our lives, and we will need to be vigilant and intentional if we care to resist. While it is undeniable and natural for us all to be consumers to some extent, Jesus reminds us that God has created us to be something more, namely *givers*, for "it is more blessed to give than to receive" (Acts 20:35). Yet how do we avoid succumbing to the stranglehold of materialism, with its obsession toward the consumption and accumulation of "stuff"? Even if we are not so crass as to make a game of acquiring things or wealth and bragging about it on a bumper sticker, any honest self-examination must go deeper and consider how we *actually live* our lives.

With regard to the accumulation of material possessions, Jesus said,

"Watch out! Be on your guard against all kinds of greed; life does not consist in an abundance of possessions." And he told them this parable: "The ground of a certain rich man yielded an abundant harvest. He thought to himself, 'What shall I do? I have no place to store my crops.' "Then he said, 'This is what I'll do. I will tear down my barns and build bigger ones, and there I will store my surplus grain. And I'll say to myself, 'You have plenty of grain laid up for many years. Take life easy; eat, drink and be merry.' "But God said to him, 'You fool! This very night your life will be demanded from you. Then who will get what you have prepared for yourself?' "This is how it will be with whoever stores up things for themselves but is not rich toward God." (Luke 12:15–21)

This passage is often referred to as the parable of the "rich fool," and some might question why God in the story refers to the obviously successful businessman so harshly. What makes him a "fool"? For one thing, instead of using the perishable commodity that he has acquired or even worked to produce, he is devoting his thoughts and energy into storing it for himself, apparently ignoring the fact that his life could end at any moment and his opportunity to use it will cease. Jesus' point is clear: it is utter folly to devote our lives to hoarding money or material things for ourselves because none of it can be taken with us. It all gets left behind! Therefore, one who seeks to put Jesus' words into practice must not be greedy, living his or her life as if the one who dies with the most toys wins. Put another way, a Christ-follower cannot legitimately devote his or her life to membership in the "die rich club."

Besides pointing out the folly of living our lives to accumulate something that we cannot take with us, Jesus warns that material wealth obscures recognition of our fundamental need for God. This power is so subtle that we may not even realize when it has a hold on us.

> A certain ruler asked him, "Good teacher, what must I do to inherit eternal life?" "Why do you call me good?" Jesus answered. "No one is good—except God alone. You know the commandments: 'You shall not commit adultery, you shall not murder, you shall not steal, you shall not give false testimony, honor your father and mother.'" "All these I have kept since I was a boy," he said. When Jesus heard this, he said to him, "You still lack one thing. Sell everything you have and give to the poor, and you will have treasure in heaven. Then come, follow me." When he heard this, he became very sad, because he was very wealthy. Jesus looked at him and said, "How hard it is for the rich to enter the kingdom of God! Indeed, it is easier for a camel to go through the eye of a needle than for someone who is rich to enter the kingdom of God." (Luke 18:18–25)

Lest we think that this teaching is directed simply at the rich ruler in the story or some other rich people, consider his listeners' incredulous reaction: "Who then can be saved?" (Luke 18:26), and Peter's protest: "We have left all we had to follow you" (Luke 18:28), which probably originated from their common Old Testament concept that a rich person, in contrast to one who was poor, had more money than needed to acquire food for today, and more clothes than those on his or her back. That is why there are direct warnings against holding a poor person's cloak overnight as loan security or withholding a poor worker's wages at day's end:

> Return their cloak by sunset so that your neighbor may sleep in it ... Pay them their wages each day before sunset, because they are poor and are counting on it. (Deuteronomy 24:13–15)

In any case, Jesus' listeners and disciples clearly understood that *they were all included* in his pointed warning to rich people.

So why on earth would Jesus say to them (and us all) that it is hard for the rich to enter God's kingdom? Because, as he stated at the start of his sermon on the hill, the kingdom belongs to those who are "poor in spirit" (Matthew 5:3), that is, those who recognize their *need for God* (who is Spirit) and their own spiritual bankruptcy in meeting that need. Material wealth can easily blind us to that reality.

Think about it: it is when times are tight, my resources are depleted, and I am not sure how I will make ends meet, or pay that medical expense or tuition bill, that I find myself consciously depending on God. When I am flush with cash, however, and my emergency and rainy-day accounts are all funded, I tend to think I can handle whatever contingencies life throws at me. Inherent in having riches is a powerful temptation to depend on them instead of God. That is why in the New Testament *greed* is equated with *idolatry* (Colossians 3:5). As Jesus said,

> No one can serve two masters. Either you will hate the one and love the other, or you will be devoted to the one and despise the other. You cannot serve both God and money. (Matthew 6:24)

Something inevitably happens to us whenever we try to serve two masters. When we allow riches, or *any*thing or anyone else, to occupy that place in our lives that only our Creator should occupy, we change. I am referring to that place in the core of our beings from which we make decisions about how to devote our time, energy or resources—literally, how each of us will live our own lives. If this virtual throne of my life is not surrendered to God, then it will be occupied by something or someone else (including possibly myself). This is what idolatry is: allowing that which is *not God* to occupy the place in my life that only God should occupy. There is no more fundamental and repeated warning in all of scripture than to flee from such "idols," or created gods (Exodus 20:3; 1 John 5:21).

Idols burden us with false definitions of success and failure (Keller 2008). Therefore, when idolatry creeps in, our definition of what it means to be a success or failure in life will certainly change. If money is my god, for example, then I am a success if I acquire it at the levels I desire, and I am a failure if I do not. I have a friend who made quite clear upon graduation from college that he was committed to becoming fabulously wealthy, a multimillionaire. Success for him, by his own definition, was therefore quite simple to determine. If he could achieve the riches to which he would devote his life, then he would be a success, and if he could not, then he would be a failure. He did not, and learned along the way that money, like any false god, is cold and unforgiving.

We must also understand that if I have made the acquisition of wealth the god of my life, as in our example, it is no small thing when I fail to acquire it. I have not just failed in achieving a goal, but I have failed in the pursuit of that which defines the very purpose and meaning of my life. My failure goes to the foundation upon which I have built my life, and with that gone, as Jesus observed, the inevitable storms of life will cause me to fall "with a great crash" (Matthew 7:27).

But the change in me caused by my pursuit of a false god such as money goes beyond my definition of success. It also changes the values I hold. I will begin to value doing those things or associating with those people that will help me accumulate money. I may find that spending time at the office or with my boss or clients has a direct impact on the money I make, so I begin to value that more and, consequently, value spending time with my family less. Over time, the scales may tip so heavily in that direction that my wife and kids could accurately say, "You're never home anymore." But I may even say to them, myself or others, completely oblivious to the irony, that I am doing this *for* my family!

With my values changing, I find that the laws by which I live my life will also change. Whereas before committing my life to the pursuit of money I might have been scrupulous in accurately filling out my timesheets or expense reports, I now may start to fudge more and be less attentive or accurate. And, if frustrated about the pace at which I can accumulate the money I crave, or my prospects of getting it legitimately, I may hypothetically start to "borrow" from a client's trust fund or cheat on my income taxes. I may even convince myself that it is okay to swindle, steal, embezzle, lie, cheat, or even murder, because doing so appears to be the best path at the moment to acquire money. Before I know it, I have changed as a person. My bearings are altered and I think and feel differently than before. I have also gone further down a path than I ever thought I would go, often with disastrous results.

Some of us may recognize these or similar stories with an uncomfortable familiarity. But whether or not they represent truths about our own journeys, there is no denying that they are realistic scenarios. We can read about them in our news sources every day.

The fact is that the gods of our idolatry, whether money or any other, will inevitably be exposed as false and unworthy of our trust. With respect to wealth, it may take a recession, or downturn in the market, or the experience of being defrauded by a trusted money manager, to remind us of that. And even if I do acquire all the money I crave, I may come to realize that I am still unfulfilled. History is full of true stories of fabulously wealthy people who died unhappy, mired in dysfunction and tragedy, in spite of having successfully attained that to which they devoted their lives. Riches, as any false god, will ultimately let us down. As St. Augustine confessed after experiencing his early affluent life, "You have made us for yourself, O Lord, and our hearts are restless until we find our rest in you" (Augustine, *Confessions* I, 1). A Christ-follower recognizes that we must put our trust in God, not money.

Instead of hoarding money or things, we must understand that whatever we have is a blessing from God to be used, while we have it, for His purposes. That is what it means to be "rich towards God," which calls to mind what Jesus surely knew—the psalmist's proclamation that it all belongs to God anyway: "The earth is the LORD's, and everything in it, the world, and all who live in it" (Psalm 24:1). People seeking to live life Jesus' way will not hoard riches, but rather will use them as a resource in our work for God's kingdom. Elsewhere, Jesus described this as an investment with dividends beyond this world:

> Do not store up for yourselves treasures on earth, where moths and vermin destroy, and where thieves break in and steal. But store up for yourselves treasures in heaven, where moths and vermin do not destroy, and where thieves do not break in and steal. For where your treasure is, there your heart will be also. (Matthew 6:19–21)

The martyred missionary, Jim Elliot, once wrote in his journal that "he is no fool who gives what he cannot keep, to gain that which he cannot lose" (Jim Elliot 1949, 174). Indeed, money can be a powerful resource in our calling to bring heaven to earth, and earth to heaven (Matthew 6:10).

Focus for a moment on Jesus' statement that "where your treasure is, your heart will be also." That seems *counterintuitive* because one would think that we will put our money in the things we love. But Jesus is right-on about our character—where our money is, *there we will devote our love and attention*. If you doubt that, then place a bet on a game next week and pick a team that you otherwise care nothing about. Or buy into the Derby pool at your neighbor's house next May and pick a horse that you have never heard of. You will suddenly become intensely interested in the game or race, yelling at the TV for your newfound team or horse to win. You will experience genuine elation if they do, or the agony of defeat if they do not. That is because your heart follows your treasure. This truth also means that when we invest our money for God's purposes, our love and attention will be focused there. For that reason, such investments are wise and will help keep us from allowing money to become our god.

A Christ-follower must take deliberate steps to make sure that money does not become his or her god. Such steps taught by Jesus include not hoarding money or the things it can buy, not depending on our riches instead of God, and recognizing our financial resources as a blessing from God to be used in our work for His kingdom.

Principle 11: Don't be greedy, hoarding money or things.

CHAPTER 13

Being Generous

One life, but we're not the same
We get to carry each other, carry each other
—U2

If you live near a big city, chances are that you have had the experience of a scruffy looking person approaching you on the street and asking for money. Where I live, there is a pretty little downtown area called Hemming Plaza that sits right outside the front door of two major halls of power—city hall and the federal courthouse. Much to the chagrin of the local authorities and surrounding businesses, the homeless tend to congregate there, and it would be unusual to pass through or spend a few moments in Hemming Plaza without a person, obviously down on his luck, asking you for money. There has been an outcry by local merchants and downtown development organizations to do something about the situation, and it has made for some unusual news items, such as the time when a church group was ticketed by local police for feeding the homeless.

Even outside downtown areas of a city, I have had the recurring experience of being approached in the parking lot of a retail store by various individuals who all seem to need "bus fare for me and my girlfriend (not seen), who is pregnant, to get back home (out of state) where we can get her to the doctor," or some variation of that sad story. I confess that I have had various responses to the situation over the years, sometimes giving and sometimes not, sometimes walking quickly away, and other times taking a moment to talk. The one constant element in all these experiences, however, is that the following words of Jesus reverberate loudly in my head:

> Give to the one who asks you, and do not turn away from
> the one who wants to borrow from you. (Matthew 5:42)

Believe me, I know all of the explanations why we should *not* give to the panhandler on the street and have at times used every one. Besides the fear of being swindled, the most common one that I hear in church circles is "they'll just use it to buy drugs or alcohol." Maybe they will, but that is between them and God, isn't it? How does that get me out of the conundrum caused by Jesus' simple statement to give when asked? While I recognize that tragedies, brokenness, and addiction often result from substance abuse, each of us must ultimately decide for ourselves how to address this common situation.

Personally, I have gotten to the point where I will almost always give something if I can—usually money, but sometimes other resources like my time, abilities, and effort. I decided that I would rather err on the side of doing what Jesus said and risk being taken advantage of than not, especially when I read the Bible and see a passage like this which seems less critical of substance use and abuse by the poor and needy than we often are:

> Let beer be for those who are perishing, wine for those
> who are in anguish! Let them drink and forget their
> poverty and remember their misery no more. Speak up
> for those who cannot speak for themselves, for the rights
> of all who are destitute. Speak up and judge fairly; defend
> the rights of the poor and needy. (Proverbs 31:6–9)

Those are not verses that you see framed and hanging on many church walls! Moreover, Jesus' simple statement to give when asked seems unqualified, and if he is who he claimed to be, he seems eminently qualified to make it.

Jesus also had a lot to say about to whom we should give. He said it was very, very important—a life-and-death kind of importance—that his followers do what we can to meet the needs of the poor, vulnerable, disenfranchised and marginalized—those he called the "least of these brothers and sisters of mine" (Matthew 25:40). In some way that we do not fully understand, Jesus regards our treatment of the hungry, thirsty, naked, sick, strangers, and prisoners as our treatment of him. He said the same thing about children:

> He took a little child whom he placed among them. Taking the child in his arms, he said to them, "Whoever welcomes one of these little children in my name welcomes me; and whoever welcomes me does not welcome me but the one who sent me." (Mark 9:36–37)

If we take Jesus' words seriously, it would be very difficult to look at the poor, needy, or vulnerable among us with the same indifference as we may have before. Christ-followers most certainly must not overlook those within our reach. To do so, the apostle John wrote, reveals more about our character than we would care to admit:

> If anyone has material possessions and sees a brother or sister in need but has no pity on them, how can the love of God be in that person? Dear children, let us not love with words or speech but with actions and in truth. (1 John 3:17–18)

In the instances when I have conversed with the very poor in my path, especially some among the ranks of the homeless (those who are not in the throes of debilitating mental illness), I have found such talks to be delightful and genuinely appreciated by both of us. It is hard for me to imagine what it is like for them to be constantly treated with disdain, derision and abuse, but it is unmistakable how meaningful some real, human conversation containing a few kind, encouraging words can be, and clear that this can help fill an "emotional tank" that may be long empty.

Nevertheless, it is I who seem to be most affected and changed by such interactions, and maybe that is a part of what Jesus is teaching us. Perhaps a reason that Jesus said we will always have the poor with us (Matthew 26:11) is because, in addition to their intrinsic value as people created by God, *we need them* to teach us about ourselves and to provide a "proving ground" for the genuineness of our professed faith and love of God.

The kind of generosity that Jesus requires of his followers is less about *how much* we might have and more about doing what we can with *however much* we may have. This is illustrated in Jesus' story about the man who went on a trip and left his three employees with differing amounts of money (Matthew 25:14–30). It is only the employee who did nothing with his bag of gold that caught the man's angry disapproval when he returned. As to the other two, both of whom used their differing amounts for their employer's purposes, the man said: "Well done, good and faithful servant! You have been faithful with a few things; I will put you in charge of many things. Come and share your master's happiness!" (Matthew 25:21, 23) The same affirmation and praise is given to both employees, whether they had five or ten bags of gold.

We sometimes act as if we will start giving, or tithing, when we just get enough money. However, the amount we have is not what is important; it is being faithful with what we *do* have. That means that all of us, whether rich, poor, or middle class, are accountable for using whatever resources we have in the advancement of God's kingdom. No one is immune from Jesus' call to give.

Jesus also taught that giving *sacrificially* counts more in his eyes than giving out of one's abundance, even if the amount given is less by comparison.

> Jesus sat down opposite the place where the offerings were put and watched the crowd putting their money into the temple treasury. Many rich people threw in large amounts. But a poor widow came and put in two very small copper coins, worth only a few cents. Calling his disciples to him, Jesus said, "Truly I tell you, this poor widow has put more into the treasury than all the others. They all gave out of their wealth; but she, out of her poverty, put in everything—all she had to live on." (Mark 12:41–44)

Sometimes we may feel like we are down to our last cent. For some of us, that may be literally true. Even then, we must do what we can. We may never see the ultimate impact of giving a bit of our time, a portion of our skills and energy, or our "two small coins," but it may reach further than we can imagine. Jesus' recognition that the sacrificial gift of the widow was "more than all the others" is not only true in principle, it is also probably literally true when you consider all the giving that her example has inspired since Jesus shared her story. If we are to follow Jesus, our generosity must embody the kind of sacrifice which he taught and demonstrated, both in his life and in his death.

As Jesus' example also shows, our mandate to give generously extends beyond the poor and includes more than just our financial resources. Rather, we are to be generous givers of our time, energy, attention, thoughtful words, skills, talents, and acts of kindness to whomever God, in His sovereignty, brings across our paths or within our reach. That would usually start with our families and move outward toward neighbors, classmates, coworkers, and others in our communities. It would include waiters, store clerks, gas station attendants, and other people who serve us, and it would most certainly include our churches engaged in equipping us to serve Christ and his kingdom. Whatever the length or breadth of our reach, Jesus calls us to extend it with generosity, looking intentionally for those who might benefit from something we could give to them. In so giving of our lives for his sake, Jesus said we will ultimately find a greater blessing and quality of life (Acts 20:35).

Principle 12: Be generous givers, especially to those who are poor, needy, or vulnerable.

No Vindication Needed

Decide what to be and go be it
—*The Avett Brothers*

The story is told of Jesus and his disciples heading toward Jerusalem but seeking to stay in a Samaritan village along the way. Jesus was, by this time, a "rock star" in those parts of the world—a *bona fide* celebrity with whom people loved to rub shoulders. His ministry was firmly established, and word of his fantastic signs and miracles was widespread. While his teaching provoked the religious people of his day, even some of them secretly followed him, and others, especially the poor and sick and even the loose-living folks who would never set foot in a church, clamored to be near him, if only to touch his robe. It is not all that different than how we act around celebrities because we convince ourselves that being around someone important somehow makes us more important.

Surely the despised Samaritans had to think fondly of Jesus, right? Even though he was Jewish, he often spoke of them as he taught the Jews. But unlike other rabbis, Jesus did not condemn their beliefs or make them the punchline of a joke; rather, he portrayed them with dignity and respect. After all, in his story about the man beaten and robbed on the road from Jerusalem to Jericho, it was not the Jewish priest or lay minister who understood how to be a good neighbor to their wounded countryman, it was only the Samaritan (Luke 10:25–37). And when Jesus healed ten lepers, most of whom were undoubtedly fellow Jews, it was only the one Samaritan who had the good manners to come back and say thanks (Luke 17:11–19).

Jesus set the tone early in his ministry when he refused to avoid Samaria on a trip but passed directly through, striking up a conversation and having a drink of water with a Samaritan woman who had a live-in boyfriend and five failed marriages. When she saw that he was someone special, she ran and got her neighbors and probably her boyfriend and brought them to Jesus, who taught some more and even stayed over with them for a couple of days (John 4:16–40). Yes, if ever there was a group of people who *owed* Jesus, it would be the Samaritans.

> He sent messengers on ahead of Him, and they went and entered a village of the Samaritans to make arrangements for Him. But they did not receive Him, because He was traveling toward Jerusalem. When His disciples James and John saw this, they said, "Lord, do You want us to command fire to come down from heaven and consume them?" But He turned and rebuked them, [and said, "You do not know what kind of spirit you are of; for the Son of Man did not come to destroy men's lives, but to save them."] And they went on to another village. (Luke 9:52–56 NASB)

It is no wonder the disciples were angry when these outcasts would not show some respect or hospitality to Jesus. Did they not know who he was? Is that any way to treat the Messiah? In their reaction, the disciples were essentially saying, "Let us send these irreverent rejects a reminder of who you are, Lord. What should it be, fire from heaven? Let us blast them, Jesus, and make them acknowledge who you are." We are not much different, acting as if Christ and his kingdom need a sensational or irresistible vindication, if not with our vociferous evangelism and Bible thumping, then perhaps through legislation or judicial decision.

But Jesus did not want or need his first disciples to vindicate him then, and he does not want or need us to vindicate him now. That is not his spirit, he says. And if we are really his followers, then we will show his spirit. The way people who do not recognize Jesus yet will have a chance is if we who claim to know him actually *follow* him, living life the way he taught and showed us: loving God above all else and honoring Him in all that we do, not holding others' wrongs against them, not being judgmental or "making a show" of our religion, not being greedy but being generous instead, keeping our word, being servant-leaders who value and pursue reconciliation when relationships are broken, trusting in God and valuing the spiritual realities of life more than all things material or physical, and loving each other like we want to be loved, for starters. Then, people will be much more likely to listen to us when we share what he taught us, and some will even come to realize that Jesus can be trusted, follow him into the waters of baptism and become his disciples, too. In any case, through us living Jesus' way, they will see who he really is —and who we really are.

If Not Now, When?

Lately it appears to me, what a long, strange trip it's been
—Grateful Dead

Early in Jesus' ministry, his unbelieving siblings tried to pressure him into going up to the Festival of Tabernacles in Judea. They said if he wanted to be a true public figure, he needed to show himself in the population center so that more people could see what he was about (John 7:2–5). His brothers reasoned that a brilliant display of power around Jerusalem during a huge religious festival was the way for him to make the biggest splash. Jesus resisted their pressure but later went secretly on his own. Even before people realized he was there, considerable chatter about him was taking place:

> Among the crowds there was widespread whispering about him. Some said, "He is a good man." Others replied, "No, he deceives the people." (John 7:12)

The differing views are not surprising, given the various claims and miracles attributed to Jesus. They show the dilemma that people have had, and will always have, about Christ given the accounts of his words and life. To say "he is a good man" means essentially that Jesus' jolting claims should be believed, while "he deceives the people" means that he should not be believed.

This passage reminds me of C. S. Lewis' famous observation in which he contends that Jesus' claims about having the power to forgive sins leave us with only three reasonable conclusions, namely that he was a liar, a lunatic, or the Lord (Lewis 2001, 53–54). Lewis seems to ignore another logical option, that Jesus was a legend, or at least did not really make the claims attributed to him, which seems to be a more popular attack by modern critics. Even so, given that the Bible is where we get our account of this person called Jesus, there still remain two fundamental options that an informed thinking person can choose: either the Jesus revealed in scriptures should be believed, or he should not be believed (whether because he was deceptive, delusional, a mythical character, or he did not really say the things attributed to him in the Bible). Each of us must make that decision for ourselves. Both options are faith presuppositions, and like Jesus' siblings, we do not come to faith by osmosis, or just hanging around the character.

In Jesus' dialogue with Nicodemus, he explained that to be a part of God's kingdom, we must each experience a spiritual birth that happens when we "*believe in him*" (John 3:16). That simple message has been repackaged and distorted into phrases like "asking Jesus into your heart," affirming "four spiritual laws," or "asking Jesus to be your personal Savior." If these descriptions help you understand what it means to "believe in him," then there may be no harm, but it seems that Jesus said it the best way. At its core, to *believe in him* must mean *believing what he said* (even if, for purposes of discussion, you contend that the Bible contains only what Jesus is *reported* to have said). That is really what we mean *any* time we say we believe in somebody, and when you boil it down further, truly believing what someone says means *living as if it is true.*

We can illustrate that in something as simple as meeting a friend or client for lunch. When you tell me you will meet me at the restaurant at noon tomorrow, my belief is demonstrated in going to the restaurant at the appointed time. By acting as if you will be there, I have given substance to what I am hoping for (Hebrews 11:1), namely that you will show up as you said. Conversely, if I waited to call the restaurant at noon to confirm whether you were there before I left, you could rightly say that I did not believe in you.

Jesus had a lot to say about *who he was* and *what he came to do.* As we have seen, the Bible records that Jesus claimed he was the Messiah promised in the Old Testament (John 4:26), God's son (Matthew 16:16–17), coequal with God (John 10:30), existing from eternity past (John 8:57–58), and having the power to forgive sins (Matthew 9:2). He also said he came to seek and save the lost (Luke 19:10), give us words from God as to how to live the abundant, full, and eternal life intended for us (John 14:24, 6:63; 10:10), lay down his life willingly as a ransom for us (Matthew 20:28; John 10:11), and be raised from the dead after he was killed (Matthew 17:22–23). Jesus further said that by believing in him, even when we die we will nevertheless live (John 11:25, 6:40), and although he remains with us in Spirit, he has gone to prepare a place for us and will receive us unto himself when we die or he returns (John 14:1–3). In its essence, *believing in Jesus means living as if his statements about who he was, and what he came to do, are true.*

The apostle Peter once wrote:

> But in your hearts revere Christ as Lord. Always be prepared to give an answer to everyone who asks you to give the reason for the hope that you have. But do this with gentleness and respect. (1 Peter 3:15)

I used to think I needed to defend God and defeat the arguments of those who were opposed to Jesus. Much of my study as a philosophy major and reader of apologetics books and resources was done to learn and be able to articulate that "perfect argument" to demolish whatever objection a critic of Jesus might offer. Now, I realize that this is neither my burden nor what Peter meant. Rather, I need to be prepared to tell anyone who asks why *I* believe in Jesus. Here's why I believe:

- When I was twelve, I heard a preacher in a church service read the words of Romans 10:9: "If you declare with your mouth, 'Jesus is Lord,' and believe in your heart that God raised him from the dead, you will be saved." Upon hearing that verse, I experienced an acute and overwhelming sense in my inner spirit that I needed to make a decision either for God (through Jesus) or against Him. It was undeniable, and I responded to that tug in my spirit, walked down the aisle of that unfamiliar church (with "knees a-knocking") and said yes even though I had little understanding at the time about Jesus or the Bible. I later followed Jesus' command and example to be baptized.

- Since that initial decision to say yes to God, I have found several times throughout my life that God has shown up in a variety of unexpected and tangible ways. Some are so unlikely that it would take greater faith for me to dismiss them as chance or coincidence, and these serve as confirmation to me that God is real and present in my life (like Jesus said).

- My lifelong study of the Bible has convinced me that it is a cohesive story, woven throughout its various books and chapters, even though written over thousands of years by numerous authors. The essential narrative is that in response to our disobedience, God in His love promised to send someone who would, at great personal cost, undo the work of our spiritual adversary and save us from our sins. The one promised would be born of a woman, from the descendants of Abraham, the tribe of Judah, and the house of King David. He would be God's Son, born in Bethlehem, who would establish and reign over a kingdom that will never end, where love prevails and justice and peace are realized, and all things are being redeemed, restored and made new.

- The Bible's account of why anything, and why *the many* things, exist, though often in poetic language, is plausible and consistent while addressing the big questions of life:
  1. Where did we come from? [God made us.]
  2. Why is there so much brokenness, pain and suffering in the world? [We sinned, deliberately choosing to disobey God and go our own way, and this is the consequence of those choices.]
  3. Can it be fixed? [Yes, God in His love sent Jesus to fix it, and through his life, death, and resurrection, and the kingdom work he has called us to join in, Jesus is redeeming and restoring people and all of creation, bringing Heaven to earth.]
  4. Where are we going? [We are heading to a time and place of peace where justice and righteousness are established, all things are made new, there will be no more sickness, sorrow, pain, or death, and we will dwell with Christ in that new heaven and earth forever.]

- The Bible's revelation about human nature—that each of us tends to elevate our own interests above the interests of others—explains our behavior and is empirically validated by human experience. Additionally, it explains the functionality and flaws of various human systems of economics and governance.

- Jesus' teachings about how we should live our lives, as revealed in the Bible, are true, effective, and lead to the joy, hope, peace, and love that he promised. Conversely, to live contrary to those teachings in the way the world prescribes leads to heartache, brokenness, evil, death, and destruction.

I read in the Bible that the Spirit is the source of this life that I am experiencing, and there is no doubt in my mind this is so. While I have had missteps and made plenty of mistakes along the way, the general trajectory of my life has been intentionally in pursuit of following Jesus, who I confess as Lord and Savior, for over forty years. There is a quality to my life experience that is different and more vivid than I could have imagined, and it is present through the ups and downs of my life.

As Jesus told Nicodemus, it is difficult to explain and somewhat like the wind, which we cannot see but know is real (John 3:8). I know what he is describing, which serves as further confirmation of my first unsteady and uncertain response to the Spirit's nudge so many years ago. The psalmist said, "Taste and see that the Lord is good; blessed is the one who takes refuge in Him" (Psalm 34:8). I have done that, and respectfully invite you to do the same.

REFERENCES

Written Works:

1. Auden, W.H. 1991. "Whitsunday in Kirchstetten" *Collected Poems*, edited by Edward Mendelson. New York: Vintage.
2. Augustine. 1993. *Confessions* I, 1, translated by F.J. Sheed. Indianapolis: Hackett.
3. Bonhoeffer, Dietrich. 1995. *The Cost of Discipleship.* New York: Touchstone.
4. Campolo, Anthony. 1994. *Carpe Diem.* Nashville: Word.
5. Elliot, Jim. 1978. *The Journals of Jim Elliot*, edited by Elisabeth Elliot. Grand Rapids: Revell.
6. Hugo, Victor. 1980. *Les Miserables*, translated by The Folio Society Limited. London: Penguin.
7. Keith, Kent M. 2001. *Anyway: The Paradoxical Commandments: Finding Personal Meaning in a Crazy World.* Maui: Inner Ocean.
8. Keller, Timothy J. 2008. *The Gospel and the Heart*, Reading 2.2 "Idols of the Heart." https://www.scribd.com/doc/50551002/0410-001-Tim-Keller-pdf.
9. Lewis, C.S. 2001. *Mere Christianity.* New York: HarperCollins.
10. Lewis, C.S. 1960. *Essay on Forgiveness.* New York: Macmillan.
11. Linn, Amy. 2015. "Forgiving Someone Who Kills Your Loved One Seems Impossible. Until it Isn't." *Sojourners*, October 30. http://www.sojo.net/articles/forgiving-someone-who-kills-your-loved-one-seems-impossible-until-it-isn-t.
12. MacDonald, George. 1990. *Knowing the Heart of God*, compiled, arranged and edited by Michael R. Phillips. Minneapolis: Bethany House.

13. Miller, Donald. 2004. *Searching for God Knows What.* Nashville: Thomas Nelson.

14. Morrow, Lance. 1984. "Pope John Paul II Forgives His Would-be Assassin." *Time*, January 9.

15. Sproul, R.C. 2015. "What Does 'coram Deo' Mean?" *Ligonier Ministries Blog*, May 27. http://www.ligonier.org/blog/what-does-coram-deo-mean/.

16. Tillich, Paul. 1963. *The Eternal Now.* New York: Scribner.

17. Yancey, Philip. 1997. *What's So Amazing About Grace?* Grand Rapids: Zondervan.

Spoken Word:

1. King, Jr., Martin Luther. 1957. "Loving Your Enemies," Audio Recording of Sermon delivered at Dexter Avenue Baptist Church, Montgomery, Alabama, November 17. http://kingencyclopedia.stanford.edu/encyclopedia/documentsentry/doc_loving_your_enemies/index.html.

2. Ryken, Philip G. 2014. Wheaton College (IL) Alumni Dinner, Speech, Orlando, Florida, March 7.

Songs (in order of reference):

1. Neil Diamond, "I'm a Believer" (*More of the Monkees*, Colgems 1967)

2. Pierce Pettis, "You Move Me" (*Making Light of It*, Compass 1996)

3. Jon Anderson and Chris Squire, "Your Move" (*The Yes Album*, Atlantic 1971)

4. T-Bone Burnett, "The Power of Love," (*Truth Decay*, Takoma 1980)

5. Bob Dylan, "License to Kill," (*Infidels*, Columbia 1983)

6. Don Henley, "The Heart of the Matter" (*The End of the Innocence*, Geffen 1989)

7. Bob Marley, "Judge Not" (Beverley's 1962)

8. Carly Simon, "You're So Vain" (*No Secrets*, Elektra 1972)

9. Bruce Cockburn, "A Dialogue with the Devil (*Circles in the Stream*, remastered, Rounder, 2005)
10. Mark Knopfler, "Why Worry?" (*Brothers in Arms*, Warner Bros. 1985)
11. Pete Byrne and Rob Fisher, "Promises, Promises" (*Burning Bridges*, EMI 1983)
12. Joe Strummer and Mick Jones, "Know Your Rights" (*Combat Rock*, Epic 1982)
13. Paul McCartney and John Lennon, "We Can Work it Out" (Capitol 1965)
14. Bob Dylan, "Gotta Serve Somebody" (*Slow Train Coming*, Columbia 1979)
15. U2, "One" (*Achtung Baby*, Island 1992)
16. The Avett Brothers, "Headful of Doubt/Road Full of Promise" (*I and Love and You*, American 2009)
17. Jerry Garcia, Bob Weir, Phil Lesh and Robert Hunter, "Truckin" (*American Beauty*, Warner Bros. 1970)

ADDENDUM

Principles of Jesus' Way

Principle 1: Love God above all else—consider Him in all that you do.

Principle 2: Love others—seek their good, whether or not you feel like it or they do the same, and even if it costs you.

Principle 3: Forgive others—don't hold their wrongs against them.

Principle 4: Instead of judging others and focusing on their faults, address your own.

Principle 5: Don't make a show of your religion or bring attention to your own good deeds.

Principle 6: Value the spiritual realities of life even more than material or physical realities.

Principle 7: Instead of worrying about the future, material things or that which you cannot control, trust that God loves you and will provide.

Principle 8: Be a person of your word.

Principle 9: Instead of demanding your own rights, serve others.

Principle 10: Lovingly confront and address relational conflict.

Principle 11: Don't be greedy, hoarding money or things.

Principle 12: Be generous givers, especially to those who are poor, needy, or vulnerable.

"If you love me, keep my commands."—Jesus